Contents

Introduction

Despite the fifty odd years that have now elapsed since the outbreak of the Second World War in 1939, the effects of Nazism, both on Germany and on the world, are still very much with us. Europe's boundaries were determined at the Yalta and Potsdam conferences held in 1945. The involvement of the United States in the defence of Europe arose out of American participation in the Second World War. The state of Israel owes its existence, at least in part, to the anti-Semitic policies pursued by Hitler. The former division of Germany into a capitalist-oriented Federal Republic in the West and a communist-oriented Democratic Republic in the East was a direct consequence of Hitler's disastrous ambitions. Current disquiet in Europe about reunited Germany stems from memories of the Nazi experience.

Within Germany the need to come to terms with, and in some sense to expiate, the crimes committed during the Third Reich still imposes its own constraints. For example, in November 1988 the Speaker of the German *Bundestag*, Philip Jenninger, was forced to resign following a speech in which he sought to explain Hitler's popularity: 'Most Germans, from the middle class as well as the workers, could be convinced in 1938 that in Hitler they could glimpse the greatest statesman of our history' (the *Guardian*, 12 November, 1988).

It has also been argued that Nazi Germany anticipated many of the features of the contemporary world: 'a concern with social equality and mobility (though not including women), eradication of social obstacles to development, promotion of a secular outlook, the conquest of unemployment, attention given to the impact of development on the environment. The regime that gave us the *Volkswagen* and the *Autobahn* also made its signal contribution to the theory and practice of one party rule, political education through propaganda, youth movements, the secret police and the concentration camp, and other aspects of the apparatus of modern states in the era of mass political awareness that flourishes today' (H. Bull (ed.), *The Challenge of the Third Reich*, 1986, p. 15).

For all these reasons an understanding of the Nazi period in German history is essential to an understanding of the world as it is today.

7.50

Gower College Swansea

Gorseinon : Swansea : SA4 6RD Tel: (01792) 890731
This resource is **YOUR RESPONSIBILITY** and is due for
return/renewal on or before the last date shown.

CLASS NO.   **ACC. NO.**

1 0 NOV 2015

0 1 MAR 2016

RETURN OR RENEW - DON'T PAY FINES

CAMBRIDGE
UNIVERSITY PRESS

Published by the Press Syndicate of the University of Cambridge
The Pitt Building, Trumpington Street, Cambridge CB2 IRP
40 West 20th Street, New York, NY 10011–4211, USA
10 Stamford Road, Oakleigh, Melbourne 3166, Australia

First published 1991
Third printing 1994

Printed in Malta by Interprint Limited.

British Library cataloguing-in-publication data
Simpson, William
Hitler and Germany. – (Cambridge Topics in History).
I. Germany. Hitler, Adolf
I. Title
943.086092

ISBN 0 521 37629 7

Author's acknowledgement

I should like to thank Brigitte Plowman and Michael and Estelle Morgan for
giving me the benefit of their experiences of Germany between the wars; the
staff of the *Institut für Zeitgeschichte*, Munich, for their help and co-operation;
John Morrill for his encouragement and support; and above all my wife,
Margaret, whose interest in Germany has fired my own enthusiasm and who
has translated those documents for which no English text is available.

NOTICE TO TEACHERS

SE

The achievement of such an understanding is far from easy. There is, first of all, the problem of evidence. In some ways the Nazi dictatorship is better documented than almost any other comparable regime. Rule by terror was grafted on to a highly efficient bureaucracy. Tyranny was imposed through the typewriter. The meticulous records kept at concentration camps provide irrefutable proof of Nazi war crimes. There was no Official Secrets Act to shroud the activities of the German High Command once the war was over, and the Nuremberg War Crimes Tribunal yielded a huge quantity of evidence. But there are significant gaps when it comes to analysing the policy-making process. One historian has even gone so far as to say: 'As dictator of Germany, Hitler is for the historian largely unreachable, cocooned in the silence of the sources' (Ian Kershaw, *The Nazi Dictatorship*, 1985, p. 4). Because Hitler's rule was so unsystematic it is still impossible to determine with certainty when or why, for instance, the decision to liquidate the Jews was reached.

Another problem, not unique to Nazism, is the variety of interpretations that have surfaced in relation to almost every aspect of the Nazi period. Scholars in Germany itself, the United States and Britain, to say nothing of the Soviet Union, have now pursued their investigations for over forty years, seeking to explain a phenomenon which had such direct and dramatic consequences for their respective countries. The literature on Nazism expands every year, and keeping pace with it is hard enough for the university specialist, let alone the ordinary student. While some of the disagreements may be attributable to the committed viewpoints of those concerned, there are perfectly genuine differences of opinion arising out of the evidence itself. Was the Weimar Republic doomed by the circumstances in which it was born, by its inherent defects, or by the impact of economic forces over which it had no control? Is Hitler to be seen as a natural successor to Bismarck and William II as an exponent of aggression and expansive German nationalism, 'the German power–state idea whose history began with Hegel, and was to find Hitler its worst and most fateful extension and application' (F. Meinecke, *The German Catastrophe*, 1950)? Or was the Third Reich an aberration, the product of a unique combination of circumstances? Was Hitler's ideology a crazy mixture of half-baked ideas, or did it have its roots in German culture and political tradition? Was his rise to power dependent on the support he received from finance capital, or rather from the victims of large-scale capitalism such as the small shopkeeper and the peasant farmer? How is one to explain the breakthrough in 1932 when the Nazi vote went up to 37 per cent? It has been suggested that 'if the party's support was a mile wide, it was at certain points an inch deep' (T. Childers, *The Nazi Voter, The Social Foundations of Nazism in Germany, 1919–1933*, 1985, p. 269), and that, contrary to popular belief, the 13 million who voted for Hitler in July 1932 did so 'not because of racialist ideology, but rather in spite of it' (M. Broszat, *The Challenge of the Third Reich*, ed. H. Bull, 1986, p. 81).

Where the Nazi regime is concerned, opinions are equally divided. Was Hitler's rule an *Alleinherrschaft* (sole rule), or was it a polycratic system with many different groups jostling for power? Controversies abound over his foreign policy. Historians such as Fritz Fischer have seen a perceptible continuity between Hitler's objectives and those of Imperial Germany, while others would deny any such connection. Some have argued that Hitler deliberately planned the war that broke out in 1939 (H.R. Trevor-Roper), others that it occurred through miscalculation (A.J.P. Taylor).

Central to the whole problem of Nazism is the relationship between Hitler and the German people. There are several aspects to this. Seen through the eyes of Hitler's biographers (notably Lord Bullock and Joachim Fest), German history between 1933 and 1945 was determined to a very considerable extent by the whims and initiatives of Hitler himself. Such was his influence, K.D. Bracher has argued, that the terms Hitlerism and Nazism are largely synonymous. Marxist historians have generally held to the view, first promulgated at a meeting of the Comintern in 1935, that Fascism (including Nazism) was the dictatorship of the most imperialist element of finance capital, and Hitler was correspondingly little more than the agent of the German ruling class.

There is controversy, too, over Hitler's popularity. Is the evidence of the plebiscites, held to approve many of his actions, to be trusted? How many Germans condoned, or were at least aware of, the policies of extermination adopted towards the mentally disabled, the gypsies, and, above all, the Jews? There is continuing debate both about the legitimacy of the opposition to Hitler when Germany was facing invasion from Russia and about the goals of those who were prepared to challenge him directly.

There is a danger that successive layers of interpretation may in the end serve to blur rather than to clarify the picture, and for that reason it is salutary to go back to original sources. The plan of the book is to investigate at least some of the problems outlined above by recourse to original documents which have a bearing on the issues raised. Chapter 1 begins with the Weimar Republic, the circumstances of its birth [1.1–1.6] and the varieties of response with which it was received [1.7–1.10]. It proceeds with an examination of the Treaty of Versailles and raises the question of whether by its association with defeat, revolution and a humiliating peace treaty, the Weimar Republic was irredeemably handicapped from the outset [1.11–1.20].

Chapter 2 is devoted to an analysis of Nazi ideology, the policy of the Nazi party, and its organisation, tactics and membership. The chapter begins with an examination of German nationalism and European anti-Semitism [2.1–2.6]. The extent to which these ideas are reflected in the early policies of the Nazi party and in Hitler's *Mein Kampf* is explored in 2.7–2.10. The tactics pursued by the party between 1924 and 1928 are dealt with in 2.11–2.15; there follows a social profile of the party, both leaders and rank and file, and the chapter concludes with various explanations of the party's appeal [2.16–2.18).

Chapter 3 is concerned with Hitler's rise to power between 1929 and 1933. It addresses the relationship between the worsening plight of the German economy during these years and growing support for the Nazi party. The chapter begins by looking at the strengths and weaknesses of the Weimar Republic during the years of its greatest stability, 1924–28 [3.1–3.6]. It considers the Weimar government's responses to the world economic crisis which hit Germany in 1929, and Brüning's assumption of dictatorial powers [3.7–3.11]. Hitler's route to the Chancellorship between May 1932 and December 1933 is then traced and the roles of those who contributed to that outcome are examined [3.12–3.18].

Chapter 4 deals with the Nazi regime at home. 4.1–4.9 raise the question of how Hitler was able to transform the Chancellorship into a personal dictatorship and to suppress all forms of constitutional opposition to his authority. The nature of his rule, polycratic or personal, is explored in 4.10–4.14. The chapter ends by examining Hitler's role in two critical areas: economic policy [4.15–4.17] and policy towards the Jews [4.18–4.24].

Chapter 5 is directed at what is possibly the most contentious aspect of Hitler's rule, his foreign policy. The long-term goals announced in Hitler's *Mein Kampf* and in his *Secret Book* are brought under scrutiny [5.1]. The extent to which Hitler's policies in practice corresponded to these goals is then examined in relation to his policy towards England and Italy [5.2–5.5], Czechoslovakia [5.6–5.11] and Poland and the Soviet Union [5.12–5.18]. The chapter concludes with an assessment of the reasons for Hitler's decision to invade Russia in 1941 [5.19–5.27].

Chapter 6 analyses German responses to Nazi rule. It examines first the dual pressures of propaganda and terror [6.1–6.7]. The views of the acquiescent majority are assessed through the evidence of plebiscites and anecdote [6.8–6.13]. The attitudes of Hitler's most committed supporters are scrutinised through their participation in the worst of Nazi crimes, the holocaust [6.14–6.18]. We look finally at the motives and methods of those who for various reasons had the courage to oppose Hitler's rule and sought to bring it to an end, often at the expense of their own lives [6.19–6.28].

A note on the sources

There is a superabundance of documentary material now available on Nazi Germany. The problem that arises in a book of this kind is to know what to select. Two criteria have governed my choice: accessibility and relevance. Where there are English printed sources available I have used them, and here let me express my debt to J. Noakes and G. Pridham, whose three-volume collection of sources, *Nazism, 1919–1945*, has proved invaluable. Hitler's speeches are readily available in the two-volume edition translated by Norman Baynes, as is *Mein Kampf* in the translation by Ralph Mannheim. Other sources have been gleaned from a wide variety of secondary works, as indicated. Through the help of the Institut für Zeitgeschichte in Munich, I have had access to all the issues of the *Völkischer Beobachter* (People's Observer), the official voice of the Nazi party. Visits to the excellent historical exhibition at Dachau concentration camp and to Hitler's mountain retreat at the Obersalzberg, above Berchtesgaden, also yielded useful material, as did the Imperial War Museum.

The second criterion, relevance, has meant that I have looked for sources directly related to the issue under consideration. This means, for instance, that I have included in the discussion of Hitler's foreign policy in chapter 5 the Hossbach Memorandum [5.6], the record of a meeting held in 1937 at which Hitler outlined his foreign-policy objectives. If it appears that I have only chosen the sources that will suit the case I want to make, I can only say that I approached the subject of Hitler and Germany with no axes to grind. My purpose has been to raise questions rather than to answer them. While the issues chosen for discussion have determined the direction of my search, they have had no bearing on the findings.

An eminent German historian, Friedrich Meinecke, who was dismissed from his position as editor of the *Historische Zeitschrift* in 1935, aptly entitled his account of the Third Reich *Die Deutsche Katastrophe*. This indeed is what it was, both for Germany and the world. Germans were urged by their President, Richard Weizsäcker, in 1985, that there could be no atoning without remembering. We are under an equal obligation, and in seeking to explain the Nazi phenomenon, we can perhaps help to prevent its recurrence.

1 The weaknesses of the Weimar Republic

The birth of the Weimar Republic

The Weimar Republic was born out of the external defeat of the German empire and the internal collapse of its system of government. The two processes were inextricably linked. The conclusion of an armistice was made conditional upon changes in the political regime and in consequence the politicians who assumed power were saddled with the responsibility, and the odium, of signing a humiliating peace treaty. It is an open question whether the Weimar Republic could ever have overcome the disadvantages which attended its birth; this is the theme of this chapter.

On 29 September, 1918 the Hindenburg Line on the Western Front was breached. Ludendorff, Chief of the German Imperial Staff, called on the civilian authorities to request an armistice. On 3 October, with the Kaiser's approval, Prince Max of Bavaria, a well-known liberal, accepted the Chancellorship. Negotiations with President Wilson of the United States were opened on 4 October and, after a lengthy exchange of Notes, armistice terms were finally agreed on 11 November. Whether the Allies would have been prepared to concede an armistice without the removal of the Kaiser is one of the issues raised by this correspondence [1.1–1.3].

While these negotiations were proceeding, the internal government of Germany came under further strain. On 30 October sailors in the German High Seas Fleet refused orders to go on a 'death ride' against the British navy. The arrest of some of the mutineers led to angry demonstrations in Kiel on 3 November, and by 4 November the city was in the hands of rebellious groups of sailors. Further violence was only prevented by the despatch of a senior Social Democratic politician, Gustav Noske, who persuaded the rebels to return to their ships. In Berlin, pressure mounted for the Kaiser's abdication. They came initially from the socialist parties, but were reinforced by Wilson's refusal to parley with 'the monarchical autocrats of Germany' [1.3]. At 11.30 a.m. on 9 November Prince Max took it upon himself to announce the Kaiser's abdication, and was himself confronted shortly after by Friedrich

Ebert, leader of the Social Democrats, the largest party in the *Reichstag*, who demanded the Chancellorship. Max, having received Ebert's assurance that he would maintain law and order, and would arrange for the election of a Constituent Assembly, willingly stepped down. But this orderly transfer of power was accompanied by more sinister events in the streets. The left-wing socialist parties, led by Karl Liebknecht, invaded the Schloss Berlin (the Kaiser's residence) and proclaimed 'a free socialist republic of Germany'. Only too well aware of the dangers of a Bolshevik-style coup, Ebert believed that his survival as Chancellor depended on the support of the army. Equally, moderate elements in the army saw in the Social Democrats the best hope of internal peace. On the night of 9 November Ebert received a telephone call from Field Marshall William Groener, which cemented this alliance [1.4]. Two days later the Armistice was signed.

Documents 1.1–1.3 are taken from the negotiations between President Wilson and the German government that led up to the Armistice. In his Note of 14 October, 1918, Wilson spelled out some of the changes in the German system of government that would have to precede any negotiations:

1.1

It is necessary also, in order that there may be no possibility of misunderstanding, that the President should very solemnly call the attention of the Government of Germany to the language and plain intent of one of the terms of peace which the German Government has now accepted. It is contained in the address of the President delivered at Mount Vernon on the Fourth of July last [1918]. It is as   5
follows: 'The destruction of every arbitrary power anywhere that can separately, secretly, and of its single choice disturb the peace of the world; or if it cannot be destroyed, at least its destruction to virtual impotency . . . The President feels bound to say that the whole process of peace will, in his judgment, depend on the definiteness and the satisfactory character of the guarantees which can be given in   10
this fundamental matter. It is indispensable that the Governments associated against Germany should know peradventure with whom they are dealing.'

Messages and Papers of the Presidents, vol. XVII, 1925, p. 8906

To this the German government replied on 20 October:

1.2

In the future no government can take or continue in office without possessing the confidence of the majority of the Reichstag. The responsibility of the Chancellor of the Empire to the representation of the people is being legally developed and safeguarded. The first act of the new government has been to lay before the

Reichstag a bill to alter the Constitution of the Empire, so that the consent of the   5
representatives of the people is required for decisions on war and peace.

Messages and Papers of the Presidents, vol. XVII, 1925, p. 8608

This was still not good enough for Wilson, who replied on 23 October:

1.3

It is evident that the German people have no means of commanding the
acquiescence of the military authorities of the Empire in the popular will; that the
power of the King of Prussia to control the policies of the Empire is unimpaired;
that the determining initiative still remains with those who have hitherto been the
masters of Germany . . . If it [the Government of the US] must deal with the   5
military masters and the monarchical autocrats of Germany now, or if it is likely to
have to deal with them later in regard to the international obligations of the German
Empire, it must demand, not peace negotiations, but surrender.

Messages and Papers of the Presidents, vol. XVIII, 1925, p. 8610

After Ebert assumed the Chancellorship on 9 November, he received a
telephone call from Field Marshal Groener, First Quartermaster General of
the Army, who was ringing from the Supreme Command at Spa in Belgium.
According to his reminiscences, Groener announced the Kaiser's intention to
go into exile in Holland. The army would be marched back into Germany on
conclusion of the Armistice under Hindenburg, and there was tacit recognition
of the new German government. The conversation continued as follows:

1.4

There was an awkward silence, which was cautiously broken by Ebert. 'And what
do you expect from us?' the Chancellor asked.
'The Field Marshal expects the government to support the officer corps in
maintaining discipline and strict order in the Army. He expects that the Army's
food supplies will be safeguarded and that any disruption of rail traffic will be   5
prevented.'
'What else?'
'The officer corps expects that the imperial government will fight against
Bolshevism and place itself at the disposal of the government for such a purpose.'
So great was Ebert's relief that he could only ask Groener to 'convey the thanks of   10
the government to the Field Marshal'. And then the conversation was over. The
ultimate compromise had been secretly concluded.

Lebenserrinerungen, p. 467, Wilhelm Groener, 1957, cited in Richard M. Watt,
The Kings Depart, 1973, p. 224

Questions

1 What did Wilson mean by 'arbitrary power' in **1.1, line 6**?
2 What was the constitutional significance of the bill laid before the *Reichstag* in **1.2**?
3 What were the implications of the Note addressed to the German government by Wilson on 23 October 1918 [**1.3**]?
4 In your opinion, what effects were Wilson's conditions likely to have on any subsequent regime in Germany?
5 How would you assess the reliability of **1.4** as a piece of evidence?
6 'Thus, in half a dozen sentences over a telephone line, a pact was concluded between a defeated army and a tottering semi-revolutionary regime [**1.4**]; a pact designed to save both parties from the extreme elements of a revolution but, as a result of which, the Weimar Republic was doomed at birth' (J. Wheeler-Bennett, *The Nemesis of Power*, 1954). Why do you think Wheeler-Bennett drew this inference from the pact between Ebert and Groener and was he justified in doing so?

Despite the agreement with Groener, Ebert's position was still far from secure. On 29 December the Independent (left-wing) Socialists resigned from his cabinet, and on 5 January a Revolutionary Committee, representing shop stewards, Independent Socialists and Communists, voted to seize power. The coup was led by Karl Liebknecht and Rosa Luxemburg, members of the self-styled Spartacist League. But whereas the Bolsheviks had succeeded in Petrograd in November 1917, the Spartacists failed in Berlin. Liebknecht was no Lenin, and Ebert was no Kerensky. After a week of street fighting the rising was over. Order was restored, but in the process over one hundred workers were killed, and Ebert had to rely on units of the *Freikorps*, independently organised groups of ex-servicemen, who acquired a justified reputation for brutality and chauvinism.

Arrangements for the election of a Constituent Assembly went ahead, nonetheless, and this took place on 19 January, 1919. The Assembly convened on 6 February at Weimar, a quiet provincial town associated with Germany's greatest poet, Goethe. Forty sessions were held during which the text of the Constitution was hammered out. Its main architect was Hugo Preuss, Minister of the Interior in the Ebert cabinet, and prior to that Professor of Constitutional law at the Commercial University at Berlin.

Preuss was a member of the German Democratic Party, founded in 1918 by liberal intellectuals, and a firm believer in individual liberties and parliamentary democracy. His hopes and fears are well reflected in a speech he made to the Weimar Assembly on 8 April 1919:

1.5

I have often listened to the debates with real concern, glancing often rather timidly to the gentlemen of the Right, fearful lest they say to me: 'Do you hope to give a parliamentary system to a nation like this, one that resists it with every sinew in its body? Our people do not comprehend at all what such a system implies.' One finds suspicion everywhere; Germans cannot shake off their old political timidity and   5
their deference to the authoritarian state.

E. Eyck, *A History of the Weimar Republic*, vol. I, 1967, p. 66

The Constitution is divided into two parts: Part One, which is concerned with the structure and function of the Commonwealth (*Reich* in German), and Part Two, which is concerned with the fundamental rights and duties of Germans. **1.6** reproduces some of the key provisions. The Constitution has come in for constant criticism. Some have blamed the instability of inter-war German politics on the electoral system, others have seen the provisions relating to the Presidency and the powers given to the national government over the states as a vital stepping stone to Nazi dictatorship.

1.6   The Constitution of the German Commonwealth [*Reich*]

Preamble

The German People, united in all their branches, and inspired by the determination to renew and strengthen their Commonwealth in liberty and justice, to preserve peace both at home and abroad, and to foster social progress, have adopted the following Constitution.   5

Part One
Structure and Function of the Commonwealth

Section I
Commonwealth and States

Article 1 The German Commonwealth is a Republic. Political authority is   10
derived from the People.

Article 5 Political authority is exercised in national affairs by the National Government in accordance with the Constitution of the Commonwealth and in State Governments in accordance with the State Constitutions. [Articles 1–6 defined these separate spheres of authority.]   15

Section II
The National Assembly

Article 22 The delegates are elected by universal, equal, direct and secret suffrage by all men and women over twenty years of age, in accordance with the principle of proportional representation . . .   20

Article 23 The National Assembly is elected for four years. New elections must take place at the latest on the sixtieth day after its term comes to an end. The National Assembly convenes at the latest on the thirtieth day after the election.

Section III
The National Presidency and the National Cabinet   25

Article 41 The National President is chosen by the whole German People. Every German who has completed his thirty-fifth year is eligible for election . . .

Article 46 The President appoints and dismisses the civil and military officers of the Commonwealth if not otherwise provided by law . . .

Article 47 The National President has supreme command over all the armed   30
forces of the Commonwealth.

Article 48 If any state does not perform the duties imposed upon it by the Constitution or by national laws, the National President may hold it to the performance thereof by force of arms.

If public safety and order in the Commonwealth is materially disturbed or   35
endangered, the National President may take the necessary measures to restore public safety and order, and, if necessary, to intervene by force of arms. To this end he may temporarily suspend, in whole or in part, the fundamental rights established in Articles 114, 115, 117, 118, 123, 124 and 153. [These rights guaranteed personal liberty, protection against unauthorised searches, the secrecy   40
of postal and telegraph services, freedom of speech and writing, the right of peaceable assembly, the right to form associations and the right to property.]

The National President must immediately inform the National Assembly of all measures adopted by the authority of paragraphs 1 or 2 of the Article. These measures shall be revoked at the demand of the National Assembly.   45

Article 53 The National Chancellor and, on his proposal, the National Ministers are appointed and dismissed by the National President.

Article 54 The National Chancellor and the National Ministers require for the administration of their offices the confidence of the National Assembly. Each of them must resign if the National Assembly by formal resolution withdraws its   50
confidence.

Part Two
Fundamental Rights and Duties of Germans

Section I
The Individual   55

Article 109 All Germans are equal before the law. Men and women have
fundamentally the same rights and duties.

Section V
Economic Life

Article 151 The regulation of economic life must conform to the principles of   60
justice, with the object of assuring humane conditions for all.

Article 156 The Commonwealth may by law, without impairment of the right to
compensation, and within proper application of the regulations relating to
expropriation, transfer to public ownership private business enterprises adapted
to socialization.   65

Article 164 The independent, agricultural, industrial and commercial middle
class shall be fostered by legislation and administration, and shall be protected
against oppression and exploitation.

R. Brunet, *The German Constitution*, translated by Joseph Gollomb, 1923,
pp. 297–339

Questions

1 What were the differences between 'a parliamentary state' and the 'authoritarian system' referred to in **1.5**? Were Preuss's fears about the attitude of the
German Right to the Weimar Republic justified?
2 How far would the goals listed in the Preamble to the Constitution have been
shared by political leaders in Britain, France and the USA?
3 Is it fair to characterise the Weimar Constitution as a compromise 'between a
core of traditional Prussian absolutism and a facade of Western parliamentarism' (G. Scheele, *The Weimar Republic*, 1946, p. 41)? Give reasons for
your answer.
4 What powers are given to the President under Article 48? What safeguards
are provided against their abuse?
5 Why do you think it was felt necessary to safeguard the interests of the
middle class?
6 To what extent does the Weimar Constitution show a bias towards
Socialism?

When the Constitution was put to the vote on 31 July 1919 it was approved by 262 votes to 75. But this majority is misleading, and it is necessary to analyse the standpoints of the various parties to see the full significance of the figures. Six main parties contested the election that was held on 19 January. Their German names, abbreviations and nearest English equivalents are given below, roughly in order from right to left in the political spectrum:

> *Deutsche National Volkspartei (DNVP)* – German National People's Party
> *Deutsche Volkspartei (DVP)* – German People's Party
> *Zentrums Partei (Zentrum)* – Centre Party (mainly Roman Catholic)
> *Deutsche Demokratische Partei (DDP)* – German Democratic Party
> *Sozialdemokratische Partei Deutschland (SPD)* – German Social Democratic Party
> *Unabhängige Sozialdemokratische Partei Deutschland (USPD)* – German Independent Socialist Party

The 1919 election produced the following results:

Party	% vote	Seats
DNVP	10.3	44
DVP	4.4	19
Zentrum	19.7	91
DDP	18.6	75
SPD	37.9	163
USPD	7.6	22
Total	98.5	414

In the division on 31 July the *DNVP*, the *DVP* and the *USPD* voted against the Constitution. 1.7–1.10 indicate the range of attitudes that lay behind these figures. The first group [1.7 (a–c)] illustrates the views of Gustav Stresemann, leader of the *DVP*, and subsequently both Chancellor and Foreign Minister between 1924 and 1929. The second document [1.8] is drawn from the recollections of Kuno Graf von Westarp, a leading member of the *DNVP*. The third document [1.9] is an editorial from *Die Rote Fahne* (The Red Flag), a Communist newspaper, dated 3 March 1919, and the fourth [1.10] is a resolution passed at the Heidelberg Congress of the *SPD*, held in 1925.

1.7(a)   An article in the *Niedersächsisches Wochenblatt* (Lower Saxony Weekly), 25 March 1919

Not the 2nd of October, when Germany's decision to request an armistice was made, but the 9th November was the death day of Germany's greatness in the world.

1.7(b)   A letter from Stresemann to a fellow member of the *DVP*, 6 January 1919

I have emphasised in almost every one of my campaign speeches that I was a monarchist, am a monarchist and shall remain a monarchist.

1.7(c)   Stresemann, the Weimar Constitution and the Treaty of Versailles

The Versailles Treaty alienated Stresemann from the Republic in more ways than one, for it was also the decisive factor in his decision to lead the *DVP* in rejecting the Weimar Constitution. In April he had been ready to drop his monarchism and reconcile himself to the Republic, but he had been willing to do this only for the sake of the expected *Anschluss* with Austria. With the adoption of the treaty his brief 5 flirtation with republicanism came to an end, since that document expressly ruled out an *Anschluss*.

These three extracts are from H.A. Turner, *Stresemann and the Politics of the Weimar Republic*, 1963, pp. 13, 30, 17

1.8   The Memoirs of Count von Westarp

From my experience the cry of 'Jew' would come from the audience at almost all political meetings when criticism was expressed of political circumstances. Besides, I was often able to notice that a sleepy meeting would wake up and the house applaud as soon as I started on the subject of Jews. Not infrequently I personally felt a more timely and important theme for discussion would have been the   5 liberation of Germany or the fight against the republican system . . .

Lewis Hertzmann, *DNVP: Right-Wing Opposition in the Weimar Republic, 1918–1924*, 1963, p. 129

1.9   *Die Rote Fahne*, 3 March 1919

Workers! Proletarians!

The hour has come again. The dead arise once more. Again the downtrodden ride through the land. The followers of Ebert and Scheidemann believed they had ridden you down . . . The 'Socialist' government of Ebert-Scheidemann-Noske has become the mass executioner of the German proletariat. They are only awaiting the chance to bring 'peace and order'. Wherever the proletariat rules, Noske sends his   5 bloodhounds . . .

Richard M. Watt, *The Kings Depart*, 1973, p. 339

1.10   Resolution passed at Social Democratic Party Congress, Heidelberg, 1925

The democratic republic is the most favourable basis for the struggle of the working class, and thereby for the realisation of socialism. Therefore the Social Democratic Party guards the Republic and seeks to perfect it.

R.N. Hunt, *German Social Democracy 1918–1933*, 1964, p. 33

Questions

1 Why does Stresemann in 1.7(a) regard 9 November 1919 as the 'death day' of Germany's greatness?
2 What were Stresemann's fundamental objections to the Weimar Constitution in 1919?
3 Why was hostility to the Weimar Republic so often linked with hostility towards the Jews [1.8]?
4 Were the charges brought in 1.9 against the Social Democrats in any way justified?
5 Would it be fair to say that of the German political parties in 1919, only the *SPD* was really committed to the Weimar Republic?

The Treaty of Versailles

The task of winning public approval for the Weimar Republic was made infinitely more difficult by the peace terms imposed on Germany at Versailles. The legitimacy of German grievances continues to be hotly debated, but there can be no disputing the universal dismay with which the peace terms were received in Germany.

Germany could also reasonably object to the way in which the Treaty of Versailles was imposed. The German government had sought an Armistice in October 1918, accepting 'as the basis for its negotiations the principles laid down by the President of the United States', Wilson's Fourteen Points [1.11(a)] and subsequent speeches amplifying them [1.11(b)]. Lloyd George and Clemenceau gave a similar undertaking, subject to the reservation that Germany would have to make compensation 'for all damage done to the civilian population of the Allies'. But when the Paris Peace Conference convened in January 1919 no German delegation was allowed to attend. The peace terms were only revealed to the German government when they were formally presented on 7 May 1919 by Clemenceau, the French Prime Minister prefacing his exposition with the ominous words: 'The time has come for the weighty settlement of our account.'

The German delegation was appalled by what it heard, but was particularly shocked by the terms relating to the Saar, Poland, Austria, armaments, colonies, war guilt and reparations [1.12(a)]. There appeared to be little or no correspondence with the Fourteen Points. The Supreme Allied War Council allowed the German government fifteen days, later extended to three weeks, to make written observations on the terms. Nearly every provision was attacked in the counter-proposals presented by the German delegation on 29 May, but virtually the only concession made by the Allies was to permit a plebiscite in part of Upper Silesia. The other German claims were rejected with contempt in a Note delivered by Clemenceau on 16 June [1.13]. Instead of a negotiated peace, the German government was faced by a 'diktat', to which it had to submit, or face the threat of an invasion.

Wilson's Fourteen Points were contained in a speech delivered to Congress on 4 January 1918, and were amplified in Four Principles and Five Particulars spelled out in subsequent speeches. 1.11(a,b) list the terms of particular relevance to Germany.

1.11(a)   The Fourteen Points, 4 January 1918

4 'Adequate guarantees given and taken that national armaments will be reduced to the lowest point consistent with domestic safety.'
5 'A free, open-minded and absolutely impartial adjustment of colonial claims based upon a strict observance of the principle that in determining all such questions of sovereignty the interests of the population concerned must have equal   5
weight with the equitable claims of the Government whose title is to be determined.'
7 Belgium to be evacuated and restored.
8 France to be evacuated, the invaded portions 'restored' and Alsace-Lorraine to be returned to her.   10
10 'The peoples of Austria Hungary . . . to be accorded the freest opportunity for autonomous development.' [Later modified to provide for complete independence.]
13 Independent Polish state to be erected 'which should include territories inhabited by indisputably Polish populations, which shall be assured a free and secure access to the sea'.

H. Nicolson, *Peacemaking 1919*, 1964, pp. 39–40

1.11(b)   Wilson's speech to Congress, 11 February 1918

There shall be no annexations, no contributions, no punitive damages. Peoples are not to be handed about from one sovereignty to another by an international

Conference or on an understanding between rivals and antagonists. National
aspirations must be respected; peoples may now be dominated and governed only by
their own consent; 'Self-determination' is not a mere phrase. It is an imperative   5
principle of action, which statesmen will henceforth ignore at their peril.

Messages and Papers of the Presidents, vol. XVII, 1925, p. 8450

1.12(a)   The Treaty of Versailles (selected terms), signed 28 June 1919

Article 45 As compensation for the destruction of the coal mines in the north of
France and as part payment towards the total reparation due from Germany for the
damage resulting from the war, Germany cedes to France in full and absolute
possession, with exclusive rights of exploitation, unencumbered and free from all
debts and charges of any kind, the coal mines situated in the Saar basin as defined in 5
Article 48.

Article 80 Germany acknowledges and will respect strictly the independence of
Austria, within the frontiers which may be fixed in a Treaty between that State and
the Principal Allied and Associated Powers; she agrees that this independence shall
be inalienable, except with the consent of the Council of the League of Nations.   10

Article 84 German nationals habitually resident in any of the territories recognised
as forming the Czecho-Slovak State will obtain Czecho-Slovak nationality *ipso facto*
and lose their German nationality. [German nationals were entitled to opt for
German nationality but would in that case have to transfer their place of residence
to Germany within twelve months.]   15

Article 88 In the portion of Upper Silesia included within the boundaries described
below, the inhabitants will be called upon to vote whether they wish to be attached
to Germany or Poland . . .

Article 119 Germany renounces in favour of the Principal Allied and Associated
Powers all her rights and titles over her overseas possessions.   20

Article 160 (1) By a date which must not be later than March 31, 1920, the
German Army must not comprise more than seven divisions of infantry and three
divisions of cavalry.

Article 183 After the expiration of a period of two months from the coming into
force of the present Treaty the total personnel of the German Navy, including the   25
manning of the fleet, coast defences, signal stations, administration and other land
services must not exceed fifteen thousand, including officers and men of all corps.

Article 227 The Allied and Associated Powers publicly arraign William II of
Hohenzollern, formerly German Emperor, for a supreme offence against
international morality and the sanctity of treaties . . .   30

Article 228 The German Government recognises the right of the Allied and
Associated Powers to bring before military tribunals persons accused of having
committed acts in violation of the laws and customs of war . . .

Article 231 The Allied and Associated Governments affirm and Germany accepts
the responsibility of Germany and her allies for causing all the loss and damage to 35
which the Allied and Associated Governments and their nationals have been
subjected as a consequence of the war imposed upon them by the aggression of
Germany and her allies.

The Treaty of Peace between the Allied and Associated Powers and Germany,
1925

1.12(b) Germany after the Treaty of Versailles

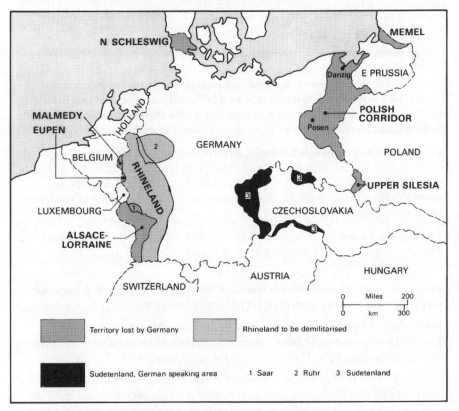

W.O. Simpson, *Changing Horizon,* **1986**

1.13 Allied response to German counter-proposals, 16 June, 1919

In the view of the Allied Associated Powers the war which began on August 1, 1914,
was the greatest crime against humanity and the freedom of peoples that any nation
calling itself civilised, has ever consciously committed . . . The conduct of Germany
is almost unexampled in German history. The terrible responsibility which lies at

her door can be seen in the fact that not less than seven million dead lie buried in   5
Europe, while more than twenty million others carry upon themselves the evidence
of wounds and sufferings because Germany saw fit to gratify her lust by resort to
war.

It is said that German Revolution ought to make a difference and that the German
people are not responsible for the policy of the rulers whom they have thrown from   10
power.
    The Allied and Associated Powers recognise and welcome the change. It
represents a great hope for peace, and for a new European order in the future. But it
cannot affect the settlement itself. The German armies had been defeated in the
field, and all hope of profiting by the war of conquest had vanished. Throughout the   15
war, as before the war, the German people and their representatives supported the
war, voted the credits, subscribed the war loans and obeyed every order, however
savage, of their government, for at any moment they could have reversed it. Had
that policy succeeded they would have acclaimed it with the same enthusiasm with
which they welcomed the outbreak of war. They cannot now pretend, having   20
changed their rulers after the war was lost, that it is justice that they should escape
the consequences of their deeds.

A. Luckau, *The German Delegation at the Paris Peace Conference*, 1941, p. 415

Questions

1 In what respects did the Treaty of Versailles correspond with and differ from
  the Fourteen Points?
2 Were the Germans justified in their objections to the territorial losses they
  suffered under the Treaty of Versailles?
3 Do you see a contradiction between Wilson's speech to Congress on
  11 February 1918 [1.11(b)] and Article 231 of the Treaty of Versailles, and
  if so, how do you account for it?
4 Compare the tone of Wilson's speech [1.11(b)] with that of the Allied Note
  on 16 June 1919 [1.13]. Account for the difference.
5 With what justification could the Allies indict the German people for
  supporting the war?

Faced with the uncompromising response to their counter-proposals, there was
a split in the German cabinet. The Chancellor, Philip Scheidemann, and the
Foreign Secretary, Count Ulrich von Brockdorff-Hentzau, favoured rejection,
as did five of their colleagues. Matthias Erzberger led the faction in favour of
signing, perhaps because he believed, quite erroneously as it turned out, that
the Allies could be induced to drop the punitive Articles. At a lengthy cabinet
meeting held on 3–4 June, Erzberger argued his case as follows:

1.14

There was no dishonour if we signed under duress, provided we announced the fact that we were signing under duress. Suppose somebody tied my arms and placed a loaded pistol against my chest, and asked me to sign a paper obligating me to climb to the moon within 48 hours. As a thinking man I would sign to save my life, but at the same time would say openly that the demand simply could not be fulfilled. The moral situation presented by [the Entente demand to sign] the treaty was exactly of the same kind.   5

Klaus Epstein, *Matthias Erzberger, A Dilemma of German Democracy*, 1957, p. 138

At 1.00 a.m. on the morning of 20 June Scheidemann resigned. Ebert finally persuaded Gustav Bauer, a fellow member of the *SPD*, to form a government, with the support of the Centre party. At Erzberger's suggestion the government proposed to accept the Treaty of Peace, subject to the following reservations:

1.15

June 22: the Government of the German Republic is ready to sign the Treaty of Peace without, however, recognising thereby that the German people was the author of the war, and without undertaking any responsibility for delivering persons in accordance with Articles 227 to 230 of the Treaty of Peace.

A. Luckau, *The German Delegation at the Paris Peace Conference*, 1941, p. 481

The National Assembly debated this proposal on 22 June. The *DNVP*, the *DVP* and the *DDP* all voted against acceptance, but it was nonetheless carried by 237 votes to 138. In the meantime, the German navy, interned at Scapa Flow, had chosen this inopportune moment to scuttle itself (21 June). The Allies were in no mood to compromise, and the German government was given to understand that it must sign the Treaty without any reservations or face invasion within a matter of days.

President Ebert made another critical telephone call to Groener. Could the army mount any effective resistance? Groener, having consulted Hindenberg, replied that it could not. Ebert advised the cabinet to comply with Allied demands. In the debate in the Assembly that afternoon it was agreed that the cabinet, as a result of the vote on the previous day, was already authorised to accept the Treaty in its entirety. To shield those who favoured signing from the obloquy that might follow, the parties opposed to signing made the following concessions:

1.16

Thus, one by one, the parties gave their declaration: Schiffer for the Democrats
[*DDP*]:
'Moreover, I hereby declare that no doubt whatever attaches to those of my friends
in other parties who, yesterday, voted "Yes".'
In the name of the German Nationalists [*DNVP*] Schultz-Bromberg said, rather   5
more vaguely, that 'The German Nationalist and People's Party lays it down as self-
understood that each member of the National Assembly voted to the best of his
knowledge and conscience'.
Heinz's declaration in the name of the German People's Party [*DVP*] rings truer:
'Of course we all of us admit that our political opponents acted, as we did, at the   10
sole instigation of patriotism.'

V. Schiff, *The Germans at Versailles, 1919*, 1930, p. 16

The Note delivered to the Allies at 5.30 p.m. on 23 June speaks for itself. It
arrived ninety minutes before Allied troops were due to march.

1.17

The Government of the German Republic is overwhelmed to learn from the last
communication of the Allied and Associated Powers that the Allies are resolved to
enforce with all power at their command the acceptance even of those provisions in
the treaty which, without having any material force, are designed to deprive the
German people of their honour. The German people, after their terrible sufferings   5
during these last years, are wholly without the means of defending their honour
against the outside world. Yielding to overpowering might, the Government of the
German Republic declares itself ready to accept and to sign the peace treaty
imposed by the Allied and Associated governments. But in so doing, the
Government of the German Republic in no wise abandons its conviction that these   10
conditions of peace represent injustice without example.

A. Luckau, *The German Delegation at the Paris Peace Conference*, 1941, p. 483

Questions

1 Was Erzberger's analogy [**1.14**] a reasonable one? Explain your answer.
2 In practice, what did the Allies achieve by their insistence on Articles
227–30?
3 In the debate on the peace terms in the National Assembly on 22/23 June,
how did the parties opposed to the signing of the Treaty of Versailles view
their opponents who were prepared to sign? Did these attitudes change
subsequently?

4 'We are perhaps lost if we do not sign the treaty, but we are certainly lost if we do sign it' (Gustav Stresemann, in an article of 14 May 1919, published in Stresemann's *Von der Revolution bis zum Frieden von Versailles*, 1919). Explain and comment on Stresemann's reaction to the Treaty of Versailles at this time.

Resentment at the Treaty was practically universal in Germany, though there were differences in the strength of opposition to particular aspects of it. The following three documents illustrate three commonly held viewpoints. 1.18 is a letter from Walter Simons to his wife. Simons was a professional diplomat who was at the time Commissioner General of the German Peace Delegation:

1.18

May 6, 1919

The Treaty which our enemies have laid before is, in so far as the French dictated it, a monument of pathological fear and pathological hatred; and in so far as the Anglo-Saxons dictated it, it is the work of a capitalist policy of the cleverest and most brutish kind. Its shamelessness does not lie in treading down a brave opponent 5 but in the fact that from beginning to end all these humiliating conditions are made to look like a just punishment, while in truth there is in them neither shame nor any respect for the conception of justice.

A. Luckau, *The German Delegation at the Paris Peace Conference*, 1941, p. 71

When the *SPD* debated the Treaty terms on 9 July 1919, the following motion was passed:

1.19

We vow today that we shall never abandon our compatriots who have been taken from us . . . unbreakable is the bond which ties us to the Germans in Bohemia, Moravia and Silesia, in Tyrol, Carinthia and Styria. In all of us lives the hope that all Germans will soon be united. We protest against the taking away of our colonies . . . the day will come when the unheard of injustices will be repealed. We shall not 5 rest in our zealous task to create the power to renounce this treaty. ·

A. Joseph Berlau, *The German Social Democratic Party*, 1949, p. 303

A popular German textbook, published by Kahnmeyer and Schulze in Bielefeld, had this to say in its last edition prior to 1933:

1.20

In the so-called peace treaty the unheard of demand for reparations and the unexampled exploitation of Germany was founded on the lie regarding Germany's war guilt. Did Germany desire the war, did she prepare it maliciously and begin it wantonly? Today every informed person inside and outside Germany knows that Germany is absolutely innocent with regard to the outbreak of war and that Russia,   5
France and England wanted the war and unleashed it.

R.H. Samuel and R. Hinton Thomas, *Education and Society in Modern Germany*, 1949, p. 75

Questions

1 What motives does Simons attribute to France and Britain in their 'dictation' of the peace terms [1.18]? Is there any justification for his accusation?
2 Locate the territories referred to in 1.19. What does this document reveal about left-wing reactions to the Treaty of Versailles?
3 What can legitimately be inferred from 1.20 about the teaching of history under the Weimar Republic in German schools?
4 'Versailles was a brave attempt to deal with intractable, perhaps insoluble, problems' (A. Adamthwaite, *The Lost Peace: International Relations in Europe, 1919–1939*, 1980). Do you agree?

2 The essence of National Socialism and the development of the Nazi party, 1920–28

In the elections to the *Reichstag* in 1928 the Nazi party gained 810,000 votes (2.6 per cent of the total vote) and a mere 12 seats. Yet by 1930 this number had risen to 6,383,000 (18.3 per cent), entitling the party to 107 seats. Such a rapid increase in support may indeed have been due to external circumstances such as the Wall Street Crash. But it could not have happened without the creation of a cadre of committed party workers, ready to seize electoral opportunity when it occurred, and the existence of large numbers of disillusioned voters, sympathetic to the ideas which Hitler was expounding. It is the purpose of this chapter to explore the ideological foundations of Nazi policies, to trace the development of the party's organisation and tactics and to analyse the sources of support on which Hitler was able to draw.

The foundations of National Socialism

The origins of National Socialism are still hotly contested. One school of thought, one of whose extreme exponents is William L. Shirer, the popular American historian, would trace National Socialism back to the rise of Prussia in the eighteenth century. Bismarck, building on the tradition of Prussian militarism, created a Prussian Germany, 'a problem child of Europe and the world for nearly a century, a nation of gifted, vigorous people in which first this man and then Kaiser William II and finally Hitler, aided by a military caste and by many a strange intellectual, succeeded in inculcating a lust for power and domination, a passion for unbridled militarism, a contempt for democracy and individual freedom and a longing for authority, for authoritarianism' (William L. Shirer, *The Rise and Fall of the Third Reich*, 1960, p. 90).

Others, of whom the contemporary West German historian Gerhard Ritter is probably the best-known example, argue, on the contrary, that 'There is no doubt that the majority of educated Germans – that part of the nation which was consciously aware of its historical traditions – was very distrustful of the Hitler propaganda which assured them that his movement was continuing and fulfilling the best traditions and hopes of German history; very many felt at the time of Hitler's victory that his political system was foreign to them' (G. Ritter, 'The Historical Foundations of the Rise of National Socialism', cited in K.D. Bracher, *The German Dictatorship*, 1973, p. 16).

What is incontestable is that Hitler drew upon a well-established tradition for at least three of his leading ideas: his belief in the superiority of the German race and its world destiny; his contempt for parliamentary democracy and his faith in heroic leaders; and his anti-Semitism, which had roots deep in European as well as German history. Before drawing too close a causal connection between the triumph of these ideas and the tradition from which they were derived, it is necessary to point out that there was a more honourable tradition represented by thinkers like Goethe, Schiller, Lessing and Kant, whose political ideals surfaced both in the 1848 Revolutions in Germany and in the founding of the Weimar Republic. There was nothing inevitable about the brief triumph of Nazi ideology. 2.1 to 2.4 have been selected to illustrate the tradition on which Hitler and the Nazis were able to draw for much of their support. There were plenty of Germans who dissented.

The first document is taken from a set of lectures delivered by the philosopher Johann Gottlieb Fichte at Berlin's Academy of Sciences in 1807–8. In 1806 the Prussian army had been humiliatingly defeated at the Battle of Jena by Napoleon, and Berlin was under French occupation at the time when Fichte gave his lectures. They helped to stimulate the revival of Prussia, which contributed to Napoleon's defeat in 1813–14, and in this way their influence was considerable, both at the time and on succeeding generations.

2.1   Johann Gottlieb Fichte, *Addresses to the German Nation, 1807–8*

You will see in spirit the German name rising by means of this generation to be the most glorious among all peoples, you will see this nation the regenerator and the re-creator of the world.

J.G. Fichte, *Addresses to the German Nation*, 1922, p. 253

To the sense of cultural destiny evoked by Fichte was added another ingredient, exemplified in the career of Otto von Bismarck: a belief in the legitimate use of force to achieve political ends. Bismarck became Minister-President of Prussia in 1862 and Chancellor of Imperial Germany from 1871 to 1890. It was under his tutelage that Germany was united between 1865 and 1871. The three wars fought in the process of unification, against Denmark in 1865, against Austria in 1866 and against France in 1870–1, were largely of his making. In the following excerpt from a speech delivered on 29 September

1862 to the Budget Commission of the Prussian Diet, Bismarck was contesting the Diet's refusal to approve an increase in the military budget:

2.2   Bismarck's speech to the Budget Commission, 29 September 1862

It is true that we can hardly escape complications in Germany, though we do not seek them. Germany does not look to Prussia's liberalism but to her power. The South German States would like to indulge in liberalism, and therefore no one will assign Prussia's role to them! Prussia must collect her forces and hold them in reserve for a favourable moment, which has already come and gone several times.   5
Since the treaties of Vienna, our frontiers have been ill-designed for a healthy body politic. The great questions of the time will be decided, not by speeches and majorities (that was the mistake of 1848 and 1849), but by iron and blood.

Emil Ludwig, *Bismarck, the Story of a Fighter*, 1927, p. 220

The way in which the German empire was established had two disastrous legacies. Bismarck's Chancellorship gave to the new German empire its authoritarian, anti-liberal character, and the military successes achieved in the course of the wars encouraged many Germans to believe in the rightness of an expansionist foreign policy:

2.3   The views of Ludwig Bamberger, a liberal Deputy in the Prussian Diet

One had to have been there to be able to testify to the power this man exerted over all those around him at the height of his influence. There was a time when no one in Germany could say how far his will extended . . . when his power was so rock-solid that everything trembled before him.

Hans Ulrich Wehler, *The German Empire 1871–1918*, 1985, p. 58

Among those who extolled the new German empire in 1871 was the eminent German historian Heinrich von Treitschke. In a pamphlet written to justify the annexation by Germany of the French provinces of Alsace and Lorraine at the conclusion of the Franco-Prussian War, he wrote:

2.4

These provinces are ours by right of the sword, and we shall dispose of them by a higher right – the right of the German nation, which cannot allow its lost children to remain forever alien to the German Empire. We Germans, knowing Germany

and France, know better than these unfortunates themselves what is to the
advantage of the peoples of Alsace, who, because of the misleading influence of the   5
French, have no knowledge of the new Germany. Against their will we shall restore
them to their true selves.

Hans Kohn, *The Mind of Germany: The Education of a Nation*, 1960, p. 164

Questions

1 In what ways do you think Fichte expected Germany to become 'the
   regenerator and the re-creator of the world' [2.1]?
2 What did Bismarck mean by 'iron and blood'? What was 'the mistake of 1848
   and 1849' [2.2, line 8]?
3 'Iron and blood has created our Reich. Iron and blood had to decide [in 1918]
   whether we could breathe freely in the world or would have to live
   henceforth in servitude and misery' (Max Lenz, Professor of History at
   Hamburg University, in an essay written in 1922). What implications can
   you draw from this remark about Bismarck's reputation in Weimar
   Germany?

The next two documents [2.5, 2.6] can be more directly linked to Hitler and
introduce a more specifically racial dimension to German nationalism.

Houston Stewart Chamberlain, born in 1855, was the son of an English
admiral. He was educated briefly at Cheltenham College (1867–70), but
following a breakdown in health studied at Paris, Geneva, Dresden and Vienna.
Germany became his adopted country. He wrote a biography of Wagner and
married Wagner's daughter. He is best known for his *Grundlagen des Neun-
zehnten Jahrhunderts* (Foundations of the Nineteenth Century), first published
in Germany in 1899, and translated into English in 1909. The book is in two
volumes and runs to over a thousand pages, but its main message may be briefly
summarised: the importance of racial characteristics in general and the
superiority of the Teutonic race in particular. Chamberlain's work was much
admired by Kaiser Wilhelm II, and Alfred Rosenberg, a Nazi ideologist, drew
on it heavily for his *Myth of the Twentieth Century*, published in 1930.
Chamberlain met Hitler in September 1923, and was so impressed that he
wrote to a friend: 'the fact that in the hour of her greatest need Germany should
produce Hitler is a sign that she is alive' (J.C. Fest, *Hitler*, 1977, p. 181). The
following excerpts from Chamberlain's book convey the essence of his
interpretation of history.

2.5   *Foundations of the Nineteenth Century*

The entrance of the Jew into European history had, as Herder said, signified the entrance of an alien element – alien to that which Europe had already achieved, alien to all it was to accomplish; but it was the very reverse with the Germanic peoples. This barbarian, who would rush naked into battle, this savage, who suddenly sprang out of woods and marshes to inspire into a civilised and cultivated   5
world the terrors of violent conquest won by the strong hand alone, was nevertheless the lawful heir of the Hellene and the Roman, blood of their blood and spirit of their spirit. But for him the sun of the Indo-European must have set . . .

At any rate it is only shameful indolence of thought, or disgraceful historical falsehood that can fail to see in the entrance of the Germanic tribes into the history   10
of the world the rescuing of agonising humanity from the clutches of the everlastingly bestial . . .

Houston Stewart Chamberlain, *Foundations of the Nineteenth Century*,
translated by J. Lees, vol. 1, 1909, pp. 494–5

A more potent and sinister influence than Chamberlain's was a mysterious publication entitled *The Protocols of the Elders of Zion*. This work has a curious and contested ancestry. According to the leading authority, Norman Cohn, whose book on the subject, *Warrant for Genocide*, was published in 1967, the *Protocols* originated in a French pamphlet, written as a satire to attack the dictatorial regime of Napoleon III in 1864. The author was a French lawyer called Maurice Joly, and he christened his work *Dialogues aux Enfers entre Montesquieu et Machiavel* (Dialogue in Hell between Montesquieu and Machiavelli). The pamphlet was published in Brussels but copies were confiscated as soon as they crossed the French border. Sometime between 1894 and 1899 a forger both plagiarised and altered the *Dialogues*, substituting the Elders of Zion for Montesquieu and Machiavelli. In its new form the pamphlet purports to describe 'lectures or notes for lectures in which a member of the secret Jewish government – the Elders of Zion – expounds a plot to achieve world domination' (N. Cohn, *Warrant for Genocide*, p.61). Responsibility for the forgery has been traced, if not conclusively, to Piotr Rachkorsky, head of the Russian Secret Police outside Russia, who was living in Paris at the time, and publication may well have been aimed to coincide with the first meeting of the Zionist National Congress at Basel in 1897.

The *Protocols* were first published in Germany in 1920 under the auspices of the Association against the Presumption of Jews. This translation went through thirty-three editions before 1933, and sold well over 120,000 copies. In 1921 *The Times* exposed the *Protocols* for the forgery they unquestionably were, and in 1935 a Swiss court declared them to be 'nothing but ridiculous nonsense'. This did not prevent Hitler from accepting them, and they were even made into a textbook by a Nazi Minister of Education. The *Protocols* preserve the form of the *Dialogues* and are extremely confused, as might be expected from their curious origins. The three excerpts in 2.6 convey the conspiratorial ambitions attributed to the Jewish race by the authors of the *Protocols*, whoever they may have been:

2.6   World conquest through world government

The Protocols of the Learned Elders of Zion

We shall create by all the secret subterranean methods open to us and with the aid of gold, which is all in our hands, a universal economic crisis whereby we shall simultaneously throw upon the streets whole mobs of workers in all the countries of Europe . . .   5

By all these means we shall so wear down the Goyim [Gentiles] that they will be compelled to offer us international power of a nature that will enable us without any violence to absorb all the state forces of the world and to form a super government . . .

It is from us that the all engulfing terror proceeds. We have in our service persons   10
of all opinions, of all doctrines, restoring monarchists, demagogues, communists and utopian dreamers of every kind. We have harnessed them all to the task: each one of them on his own account is boring away at the last remains of authority, is striving to overthrow all established forms of order. By these acts all states are in turmoil; they exhort us to tranquillity, they are ready to sacrifice everything to peace: but we   15
will not give them peace until they openly acknowledge our international Super Government, and with submissiveness.

The Protocols of the Learned Elders of Zion, translated by Victor E. Marsden, 1972, pp. 28, 37, 41

Questions

1 What contradictory role in European history does Chamberlain accord to the Teutonic race [2.5]?
2 Account for Chamberlain's popularity in certain circles in Germany.
3 What particular weapon supposedly gave the Elders of Zion their power over European economies [2.6]?
4 What role is attributed to Communists, among others, in bringing about world conquest by the Elders of Zion [2.6]?
5 How do you account for the credulity with which the *Protocols* were received (a) in Russia and (b) in Germany [2.6]?

What is the relationship between the views expressed in 2.1–2.6 and Nazism? There is no easy answer to this question. Nazism lacked a coherent ideology. It was a mishmash of ideas and policies linked only by Hitler's belief in them. It is thus in Hitler's speeches and writings, notably *Mein Kampf*, and in the official Nazi programme as interpreted by Hitler, that the essence of Nazism has to be sought [2.7–2.10]. But Hitler was not an original thinker. He drew upon a fund of ideas that he had picked up in his eclectic and unsystematic reading and upon his own experiences in peace-time Vienna and as a soldier. It is therefore to Hitler's early life that we must first turn.

Adolf Hitler was born in 1889 at Braunau am Inn, on the Austrian side of the border with Germany. His father, Alois Hitler, or Schicklgruber, was a customs officer and Hitler was the fourth child of his third marriage. Hitler was educated at the local village school, at a monastic school at Lambach and at the *Realschule* at Linz, which he left in 1905 without any formal qualifications. He applied twice to the Academy of Fine Arts in Vienna in 1907 and 1908 but was rejected both times, and he drifted aimlessly from one occupation to another in that city for the next five years. In 1913 he left Vienna for Munich, probably in order to evade his military service. However, at the outbreak of war in August 1914 he joined a Bavarian infantry regiment with alacrity, and spent the next four years on the Western Front. He was evidently an exemplary soldier, even though he did not progress beyond the rank of corporal. He won the Iron Cross, was wounded in October 1916, and badly gassed in October 1918. He was recovering in hospital near Stettin when the Armistice was declared.

He returned to the reserve battalion of his regiment at Munich in 1919, and was assigned to the 'Enlightenment Squad', designed to keep returning soldiers out of the toils of revolutionary ideas, because of his talent for political argument. It was in this capacity that he was instructed to monitor the activities of the German Workers' Party (*Deutsche Arbeiterpartei – DAP*) in September 1919.

Two main tributaries fed into the *DAP*, which subsequently became the Nazi party. The first was the anti-Semitic right-wing *völkisch* movement represented in Munich by the Thule Society (*Thulegesellschaft*), founded in October 1918 by a certain Baron Sebottendorff; the second was the left-wing workers' National Socialist movement, which originated at Trotnau in north-east Bohemia in 1904. Here the first German Workers' party was founded, primarily to safeguard German industrial workers against the competition of Czech migrants who were threatening their livelihoods. In January 1919 Anton Drexler, who worked in the Munich works of the Federal Railways, and Karl Harrer, a sports journalist who belonged to the Thule Society, set up a second German Workers' party based in Munich. Hitler first attended a party meeting on 12 September. Though only an observer, he made such a favourable impression by his contribution in discussion that he was invited to join both the party and its governing board. Hitler accepted the invitation. On 16 October 1919 he addressed his first public meeting. At the age of thirty his political career had begun.

Over the next four years the party grew steadily, as did Hitler's role in it. On 24 February 1920 the party programme was officially announced [2.7] and a new name was adopted, the *National Sozialistische Deutsche Arbeiterpartei* (usually abbreviated to *NSDAP* or *NAZI*). In December 1920 the *Völkischer Beobachter* (People's Observer) was bought and became the party's mouthpiece. In August 1921 the *SA* was founded. Initially the letters stood for *Sports Abteilung* – Sports Division – but soon came to mean the more familiar *Sturm Abteilung* or Storm Troopers, the strong-arm squads who were to act as the 'battering ram' of the party. Hitler became the party's chief propagandist. In one year alone he delivered thirty-one speeches; 2.8 provides a typical example of these. On 29 July 1921 Hitler succeeded in having his authority over the party officially recognised, and from this point on he was addressed as *der Führer*, the Leader.

2.7

Basic Programme of the National Socialist

German Workers' Party

The programme of the German Workers' Party is a static programme. The leaders reject the idea of setting new goals after the initial aims laid down in the programme have been achieved simply in order to ensure the continued existence of the party by artificially increasing unrest amongst the masses.

1. We demand the uniting together of all Germans, on the basis of the people's right of self-determination, in a greater Germany.
2. We demand equal status for Germany *vis à vis* other nations and the annulling of the Peace treaties drawn up in Versailles and St. Germain.
3. We demand land and property (colonies) to provide food for our nations and settlement areas for our population surplus.
4. Only a fellow German can have right of citizenship. A fellow German can only be so if he is of German parentage, irrespective of religion. **Therefore no Jew can be considered to be a fellow German**.
5. Those people who have no right of citizenship should only be guests in Germany and must be subject to laws concerning foreigners.
6. Only citizens should have the right to decide the leadership and laws of the state. Therefore, we demand that only those with rights of citizenship should have access to employment in any public office, whether it be at national, Länder

or local level – we oppose the corrupt parliamentary system in which people are employed only on the basis of which party they belong to and not according to their character or ability.

7. We demand that the first priority of the state should be to ensure that its citizens have a job and a decent life. If it should prove impossible to feed the whole population of the state, foreign nationals (with no right of citizenship) should be repatriated.
8. Any further immigration of non-Germans must be prevented. We demand that all non-Germans who have entered the Reich since 2nd August 1914 be forced to leave immediately.
9. All citizens must have equal rights and obligations.
10. The first duty of all fellow citizens must be to work, either physically or mentally. The actions of an individual must not run contrary to the general interest and must have consideration for the common good.

Therefore, we demand:

11. Abolition of income for unemployed people or for those making no effort.

The breaking of the dominance of invested capital.

12. With regard to the huge physical and personal sacrifice which all wars demand of the people, personal enrichment by means of war must be seen as a crime against the nation. Therefore, we demand **the collection of all wartime profits.**

13. We demand the nationalisation of all publicly owned companies (Trusts).

14. We demand profit-sharing by large companies.

15. We demand that generous improvements be made in the old age pension system.

16. We demand the establishment and maintenance of a healthy middle class. The large department stores should be immediately placed under the control of the local authority and should be rented out to small businesses at low prices. All small businesses should have the keenest regard for their deliveries to the state, the Länder or the local authorities.

17. We demand a property reform, which is in line with our requirements, and the creation of a law, which would allow the confiscation of property without compensation if this were in the general interest of the nation. We demand the abolition of all ground rents and the banning of all property speculation.

18. We demand an all-out battle against those who damage the common interest by their actions – criminals against the nation, profiteers, racketeers etc. should be punished by death, without regard for religion or race.

19. We demand the replacement of the system of Roman law, which serves the materialistic world order, by a system of German common law.

20. In order to make it possible for all capable and diligent Germans to receive a good education, thus enabling them to take up leading positions of employment, the state must carry the burden of a thorough overhaul of the national education system. The curricula of all institutions of education must adapt to the practical requirements of life. We must aim to instil national ideas from the earliest age in school (lessons in citizenship). We demand that the brightest children of poor parents should be supported by the state irrespective of their class or job.

21. The state must ensure the general good health of its citizens, by providing for mothers and children, by banning child labour, by ensuring the development of physical fitness, by making it a legal obligation to participate in sport or gymnastics and by providing all possible support for associations involved in instructing the youth in physical fitness.

22. We demand the abolition of the Söldnerheer and its replacement by a people's army (Volksheer).

23. We demand a legal battle against **open political slander** and its publication in the press. In order to make possible the establishment of a German press, we demand that:

    a) Newspaper editors and employees whose work appears in German must have German citizenship rights.

    b) Non-German newspapers must have the express permission of the state before they can appear in Germany. They must not be printed in German.

    c) Any financial contributions to German newspapers or any influence at all by non-Germans should be banned by law. Furthermore, we demand that any contraventions of the above should lead to the closing down of the newspaper in question and to the immediate expulsion from the Reich of those non-Germans involved.

    Newspapers which are deemed to be against the common good should be banned. We demand a legal battle against any art and literature which exerts a harmful influence on public life and we demand that all institutions which contravene the aforementioned standards be closed down.

24. We demand the freedom of religion in the Reich so long as they do not endanger the position of the state or adversely affect the moral standards of the German race. As such the Party represents a positively Christian position without binding itself to one particular faith. The party opposes the materialistic Jewish spirit within and beyond us and is convinced that a lasting recovery of our people can only be achieved on the basis of:

Common Good before Personal Gain

25. In order to achieve all of the aforegoing we demand the setting up of a strong central administration for the Reich.

    We demand unrestricted authority for the central parliament over the whole Reich and its organizations. We demand the establishment of professional and industrial chambers to assist the implementation of the laws of the Reich in the Länder.

The leaders of the party promise to commit themselves fully to the achievement of the above aims, and to sacrifice their lives if need be.

Munich, 24th February 1920   For the **Party Committee:** Anton Drexler

Contributions should be sent to the Head Office; **Corneliusstraße 12** (Tel. 23620)
Business Hours 9–12 (am), 2–6 (pm)

Questions on German History, Ideas, Forces, Decisions from 1800 to the Present, Historical Exhibition in the Berlin Reichstag Catalogue, 9th (updated) edition, German Bundestag and Press Information Centre, Publications Section, Bonn, 1984, p. 316

2.8   Speech by Hitler, 12 April 1922

1. 'National' and 'social' are two identical conceptions. It was only the Jew who succeeded, through falsifying the social idea and turning it into Marxism, not only in divorcing the social idea from the national, but in actually representing them as utterly contradictory.

That aim he has in fact achieved. At the founding of this movement we formed   5
the decision that we would give expression to this idea of ours of the identity of the two conceptions: despite all warnings on the basis of what we had come to believe, on the basis of the sincerity of our goodwill, we christened it 'National Socialism'. We said to ourselves that to be 'national' means above everything to act with boundless and all-embracing love for the people and, if necessary, even to die for it.   10
And similarly to be 'social' means so to build up the state and the community of the people that every individual acts in the interest of the community of the people and must be to such an extent convinced of the goodness, of the honourable straightforwardness of this community of the people as to be ready to die for it.
2. And then we said to ourselves: there are no such things as classes: they cannot   15
be. Class means caste and caste means race. If there are castes in India, well and good. There it is possible, for there there were formerly Aryans and dark aborigines. So it was in Egypt and Rome. But with us in Germany where everyone who is a German at all has the same blood, has the same eyes and speaks the same language, here there can be no class, here there can be only a single people and beyond that   20
nothing else.

The Speeches of Adolf Hitler, April 1922–August 1939, ed. Norman H. Baynes, vol. I, 1942, pp. 15–16

Questions

1 Which of the 25 points strike you as explicitly nationalist?
2 Which of the 25 points strike you as explicitly racist?
3 Which of the 25 points strike you as explicitly Socialist?
4 Explain any links you can detect between the 25 points and the sentiments expressed in 2.5 and 2.6.
5 Comment on the difference in tone between 2.7 and 2.8.
6 How did Hitler attempt to reconcile 'Nationalism' and 'Socialism' [2.8]?
7 Do you think that 2.7 and 2.8 were aimed at different audiences? If so, which was likely to have made the wider appeal?

While the Nazi party was establishing itself, the Weimar Republic sustained two damaging body blows. Between the spring of 1922 and the autumn of 1923

the monetary system collapsed and Germany endured terrifying hyperinfla-
tion. By September 1923 the exchange value of the pound was equivalent to
15 million marks. In January 1923 French troops occupied the Ruhr because of
German failure to meet reparations payments. A policy of passive resistance
was adopted which halted all coal and iron production. In September 1923
Gustav Stresemann became the new Chancellor, and announced the abandon-
ment of passive resistance in order to bring Germany's economic crisis to an
end. It was this policy of co-operation with the terms of the Treaty of
Versailles, it would seem, that confirmed Hitler's decision to make a bid for
power. On 8 November he mobilised units of the *SA* and made a violent
entrance into a meeting at the Burgerbrau Keller in Munich where the
Bavarian authorities, equally opposed to the Weimar government, were
deciding what steps to take. Hitler secured the apparent co-operation of Kahr,
the State Commissioner, General von Lossow, head of the Bavarian *Reichswehr*, and Colonel von Seisser. Ludendorff also consented to give his support to
the coup Hitler planned. That night he issued a proclamation announcing the
replacement of the existing government. But on this occasion the *Reichswehr*
stayed loyal to Weimar. Kahr and Lossow withdrew their support and on
9 November a march of Nazi party supporters, led by Ludendorff and Hitler,
was halted by police and troops. Shots were fired and sixteen Nazis were killed.
Hitler fled to the house of a friend, where he was arrested two days later. At his
trial Hitler was unrepentant [2.9(a)]. His judges were lenient, and he was given
the minimum sentence for treason, five years imprisonment. He served only
nine months, in comfortable surroundings at Landsberg Prison. It was here
that he composed the first volume of *Mein Kampf* (My Struggle). It was
dedicated to the sixteen Nazis killed on 9 November.

2.9(a) Hitler's closing speech at his trial after the Munich *Putsch*

For not you, gentlemen, will deliver judgment on us; that judgment will be
pronounced by the eternal court of history, which will arbitrate the charge that has
been made against us. I already know what verdicts you will hand down. But that
other court will not ask us: did you or did you not commit high treason? That court
will judge us, will judge the Quartermaster-general of the former army, will judge   5
his officers and soldiers, as Germans who wanted the best for their people and their
Fatherland, who were willing to fight and to die. May you declare us guilty a
thousand times; the goddess of the eternal court will smile and gently tear in two the
brief of the State Prosecutor and the verdict of the court; for she acquits us.

J.C. Fest, *Hitler*, 1977, p. 193

2.9(b)   Hitler at the Munich trial, with Ludendorff on his immediate right and Röhm on his immediate left (front row)

PERNET   WEBER   FRICK KRIEBEL LUDENDORFF   HITLER BRÜKNER RÖHM WAGNER

Weimar Archive

Questions

1 Why did Hitler expect to be acquitted by 'the eternal court of history' [**2.9(a), line 2**]?
2 Why was Hitler given such a light sentence after the Munich *putsch*, and with what justification?
3 What can you infer from **2.9(b)** about the conduct of the 'Hitler-trial'?
4 What importance did it have for Hitler's career?

Mein Kampf

Hitler dictated *Mein Kampf* to his secretary, Rudolf Hess, and to his chauffeur, Emil Maurice, though Hess's wife later insisted that Hitler had typed and edited it all himself. It is a curious mixture, part autobiography, part history. It is also a diatribe against Jews and Marxists (the two are frequently and inaccurately linked); it contains Hitler's remedies for Germany's domestic and foreign dilemmas; and it is also a shrewd political primer, with advice on propaganda and political tactics. Historians differ about the relevance of *Mein*

Kampf to the understanding of Hitler's subsequent ambitions and policies. After becoming Chancellor, he supposedly dismissed it as 'fantasies from behind bars' (A.J.P. Taylor, *A Personal History*, 1983, p. 234), and said that had he known he would become Chancellor he would never have written it. But he also said: 'As to the substance there is nothing I would want to change' (J.C. Fest, *Hitler*, 1977, p. 206). Though sales were limited to about 25,000 between 1924 and 1928, when Hitler became Chancellor on 31 January 1933 the *Völkischer Beobachter* advertised *Mein Kampf* as the Book of the Day, and urged all Germans to read it. K.D. Bracher has remarked: 'after the conquest of the state [i.e. Hitler's accession to power], Hitler's *Mein Kampf*, Rosenberg's *Mythus* and the racist–imperialist extreme literature of "the fighting years" remained for all to see and were offered up in millions of copies as official reading matter' (K.D. Bracher, *The German Dictatorship*, 1973, p. 314). This seal of approval means that *Mein Kampf* is still a vital source for understanding not only Hitler's ideas but also the ideology of the Nazi party. The following passages [2.10(a–f)] have been selected to indicate where Hitler drew upon the ideas already discussed [2.1–2.6] and the particular slant he gave to them.

2.10(a)

Mustn't our principle of parliamentary majorities lead to the demolition of the idea of leadership? Does anyone believe that the progress of this world springs from the minds of majorities and not from the brains of individuals? By rejecting the authority of the individual and replacing it by the numbers of some momentary mob, the parliamentary principle of majority rule sins against the basic aristocratic   5
principle of Nature, though it must be said that this view is not necessarily embodied in the present-day decadence of our upper ten thousand . . .

This invention of democracy is most intimately related to a quality which in recent times has grown to be a real disgrace, to wit, the cowardice of a great part of our so-called 'leadership'. What luck to be able to hide behind the skirts of a so-   10
called majority in all decisions of any real importance!

2.10(b)

What we must fight for is to safeguard the existence and reproduction of our race and our people, the sustenance of our children and the purity of our blood, the freedom and independence of the fatherland, so that our people may mature for the fulfilment of the mission allotted it by the creator of the universe.

2.10(c)

The very founding of the Reich seemed gilded by the magic of an event which uplifted the entire nation. After a series of incomparable victories, a Reich was born

for the sons and grandsons – a reward for immortal heroism. Whether consciously
or unconsciously, it matters not, the Germans all had the feeling that this Reich,
which did not owe its existence to the trickery of parliamentary factions, towered   5
above the measure of other states by the very exalted manner of its founding; for not
in the cackling of a parliamentary battle of words but in the thunder and rumbling
of a front surrounding Paris was the solemn act performed: a proclamation of our
will declaring that the Germans, princes and people, were resolved in the future to
constitute a Reich and once again to raise the imperial crown to symbolic heights.   10
And this was not done by cowardly murder; no deserters and slackers were the
founders of the Bismarckian state, but the regiments at the front. The unique birth
and baptism of fire in themselves surrounded the Reich with a halo of historic glory
such as the oldest states – and they but seldom – could boast.

2.10(d)

It is idle to argue which race or races were the original representatives of human
culture and hence the real founders of all that we sum up under the word
'humanity'. It is simpler to raise this question with regard to the present, and here
an easy clear answer results. All the human culture, all the results of art, science,
and technology that we see before us today, are almost exclusively the creative   5
product of the Aryan. This very fact admits of the not unfound inference that he
alone was the founder of all higher humanity, therefore representing the prototype
of all that we understand by the word 'man'.

2.10(e)

On this first and greatest lie, that the Jews are not a race but a religion, more and
more lies are based in necessary consequence . . .
  To what an extent the whole existence of this people is based on a continuous lie
is shown incomparably by the *Protocols of the Wise Men of Zion*, so infinitely hated
by the Jews. They are based on a forgery, the *Frankfurter Zeitung* moans and   5
screams once a week: the best proof that they are authentic. What many Jews do
unconsciously is here consciously exposed. And that is what matters.

2.10(f)

The danger to which Russia has succumbed is always present for Germany. Only a
bourgeois simpleton is capable of imagining that Bolshevism has been exorcised.
With his superficial thinking he has no idea that this is an instinctive process; that is
the striving of the Jewish people for world domination . . . in Russian Bolshevism
we must see the attempt undertaken by the Jews in the twentieth century to achieve   5
world domination.

Adolf Hitler, *Mein Kampf*, translated by Ralph Manheim, 1969, pp. 74–5,
195, 205, 263, 279, 604

Questions

1 Compare Hitler's view of Germany's historic role [2.10(b, d)] with the views of Fichte [2.1], Treitschke [2.4] and Houston Stewart Chamberlain [2.5].
2 In what respects do 2.2 and 2.10(a, c) suggest that Hitler saw himself as a natural successor to Bismarck?
3 To what extent is Hitler's anti-Semitism, reflected in 2.10(e, f), a natural extension of a European anti-Semitic tradition [2.5–2.6]?
4 What light do these passages from *Mein Kampf* throw on Hitler's personality and intellectual capacities?

Organisation and tactics, 1924–28

Hitler was released from Landsberg Prison in December 1924. During his absence the Nazi party came close to disintegration. It was officially banned, as was its paper, the *Völkischer Beobachter*. Rosenberg, who was nominally in charge, attempted to create a substitute party, the *Grossdeutsche Volksgemein-schaft* (Greater German People's Community), while Ludendorff and Gregor Strasser formed the rival *Deutschvölkische Freiheitspartei* (German People's Freedom party). Hitler would have nothing to do with either of these organisations. On his release from prison he managed to convince the Bavarian Prime Minister that he would work within the Weimar constitution, and the ban on the Nazi party and its newspaper was lifted in February 1925. On 27 February the party was officially re-founded, with Hitler as its first member.

Over the next four years he imposed his unimpeachable authority over the party, in terms of both its organisation and its policies. In February 1926, after a five-hour speech at Bamberg, where the party was meeting, he headed off an attempt by Gregor Strasser to rewrite the party programme along more Socialist lines. In May 1926 he secured a change to the membership regulations, confining the right to vote for the Chairmanship of the party to the Munich members. In July at the first party congress, held ironically at Weimar, he laid it down that only motions approved by the Leader were to be discussed. The same month he appointed Joseph Goebbels, one of Strasser's previous supporters, but now a close ally of Hitler's, to be *Gauleiter* (District Leader) in Berlin. He also appointed a new head of the *SA*, Pfeffer von Salomon. By the end of 1926, therefore, Hitler's position was unchallenged and he was able to play the role of Leader sketched out in *Mein Kampf*. 2.11–2.13 demonstrate Hitler's concept of leadership and its acceptance by the party, and his growing influence over policy.

2.11

The young movement is in its nature and inner organisation anti-parliamentarian; that is, it rejects in general and in its own inner structure, a principle of majority rule in which the leader is degraded to the level of a mere executant of other people's will and opinion. In little as well as big things, the movement advocates the principle of German democracy: the leader is elected, but then enjoys unconditional authority.   5

Adolf Hitler, *Mein Kampf*, translated by Ralph Manheim, 1969, p. 312

2.12   Report of the Annual Party Meeting, 2–3 September 1928

Above all, Hitler notes the gradual penetration of the whole movement with the basic concept of our ideas. He stresses the gradual consolidation of the leadership principle (*Führerprinzip*). The movement can be proud of the fact that it is the only one based on a logical foundation. This was necessary in order to make up for our numerical minority by a maximum degree of inner discipline, stability, fighting   5
power, in short, energy . . .

The chairman of the meeting, Gregor Strasser, expresses the mood of the meeting very well by remarking that any other party would now say that they have heard the report of the chairman, whereas we National Socialists have heard the speech of the leader. And there is the same difference between the chairman of the   10
old parties and the leader of the movement as there is between the report of the chairman and the speech we have just heard.

The party busines is now quickly dealt with according to the regulations. First 'the election of the statutory executive committee'. To the amusement of the audience, Strasser proposes *NSDAP* member Hitler as Chairman. He notes that he   15
has been unanimously elected by a show of hands *(laughter)*.

Nazism, 1919–1945, ed. J. Noakes and G. Pridham, vol. I, 1983, p. 55

2.13   Speech by Hitler, 13 April 1928

It is necessary to reply to false interpretations on the part of our opponents of Point 17 of the programme of the *NSDAP* [see **2.7**]. Since the *NSDAP* admitted the principle of private property, it is obvious that the expression 'confiscation without compensation' refers merely to the creation of possible legal means of confiscating, when necessary, land illegally acquired, or not administered in   5
accordance with the national welfare. It is therefore directed in the first instance against Jewish companies which speculate in land.

The Speeches of Adolf Hitler, 1922–1939, ed. Norman H. Baynes, vol. I, 1942, p. 105

Questions

1 How far and in what ways did the organisation of the Nazi party reflect 'the principle of German democracy' by 1928 [2.11, **line 5, 2.12**]?
2 Would it be true to say that by 1928 the Nazi party had ceased to be Socialist? Explain your answer.

While the years 1924–28 saw the consolidation of Hitler's hold on the Nazi party and its policies, they also witnessed its transformation into a movement. Various means were employed to this end. Subordinate organisations were created to appeal to particular interest groups. In 1926 the NS Students' League, Physicians' League, Teachers' League, Law Officers' League and Women's League all materialised. The *SA* continued to recruit actively. The party also adopted the uniforms, the insignia and the rituals that became its hallmark. Brown shirts, designed for German troops in East Africa and acquired from war-surplus stocks, became the party uniform in 1924. The swastika, the *Hakenkreuz* (hooked cross), became the party emblem. This symbol was derived from Norse mythology and had strong anti-Semitic associations. The party rallies held at Weimar in 1926 and Nuremberg in 1927 established the pattern of military-style parade and revivalist meeting that were to be such a feature of Nazi demonstrations in the 1930s. In part, Hitler was only imitating the practice of other parties in the Weimar Republic. The Nationalists had their *Stahlhelm* (Steelhelmet) and the Social Democrats their *Reichsbanner Schwarz-Rot-Gold* (Imperial flag, black, red, gold, the colours of the Weimar Republic), paramilitary organisations used to defend their meetings. But what distinguished Nazi tactics was their use of democratic weapons to undermine democracy. Though Hitler had deliberately abandoned the military route to power after the failure of the Munich *putsch* in 1923, neither he nor his supporters showed anything but contempt for the democratic process, as **2.14–2.15** indicate.

2.14   The policy of legality, a conversation with Hitler in the fortress at Landsberg, 1924

When I resume active work it will be necessary to pursue a new policy. Instead of working to achieve power by an armed *coup* we shall have to hold our noses against the Catholic and Marxist deputies. If out-voting them takes longer than out-shooting them, at least the results will be guaranteed by their own Constitution! . . . Sooner or later we shall have a majority – and after that, Germany. I am convinced   5 that this is our best line of action, now that conditions in the country have changed so radically.

Kurt G.W. Ludecke, *I Knew Hitler*, 1938, p. 218

2.15   Joseph Goebbels, *Der Angriff* (The Attack), 30 April 1928: 'What do we want in the *Reichstag*?'

We go into the *Reichstag* in order to acquire the weapons of democracy from its arsenal. We become *Reichstag* deputies in order to paralyse the Weimar democracy with its own assistance. If democracy is stupid enough to give us free travel privileges and *per diem* allowances for this purpose, that is its affair . . . We'll take any legal means to revolutionise the existing situation . . . Mussolini also went into   5 parliament, yet soon thereafter he marched into Rome with his Blackshirts . . . One should not believe that parliamentarism is our Damascus. We come as enemies! Like the wolf tearing into the flock of sheep, that is how we come. Now you are no longer among yourselves.

K.D. Bracher, *The German Dictatorship*, 1973, pp. 182–3

Questions

1 What can you infer from **2.14** and **2.15** about Nazi views of the democratic process?
2 Why do you think the Weimar governments allowed articles such as **2.15** to be published? Should they have done so?

Nazi party supporters

On the face of it, Hitler's tactics were failing in 1928. Whereas in May 1924 the German People's Freedom Party, which temporarily replaced the banned Nazi party, gained 1.9 million votes, and 32 seats in the *Reichstag*, the Nazi vote in 1928 fell to 810,000, entitling them to a mere 12 seats. Yet among these 12 were the future leaders of the Third Reich: Göring, Frick and Goebbels. Membership of the party had risen from 27,000 in 1925 to over 100,000 in 1928, and, as Bracher writes, 'The 100,000 strong *NSDAP*, unlike the *putschist* party of 1923, controlled tightly knit cadres in all parts of Germany which, with the approaching economic crisis, stood ready to branch into a mass organisation' (K.D. Bracher, *The German Dictatorship*, 1973, p. 172). From where were these enthusiasts drawn? Various efforts have been made to identify the typical Nazi. Here three kinds of evidence will be cited: a composite portrait of the Nazi leadership as it was in 1928 [2.16]; a sociological analysis based on party membership lists in nine different areas [2.17]; and the responses to an enquiry commissioned by an American sociologist, Theodore Abel, in 1934, in which a prize was offered 'for the best personal life history of an adherent of the Hitler movement' [2.18].

2.16   A portrait of the Nazi leadership

Name	Born	Social background	War/Career
M. Bormann	1900	Lower middle class	Served in ranks; joined *Freikorps* in Rossbach
G. Feder	1883	Lower middle class	Engineer/Economist
W. Frick	1877	Lower middle class	Senior Police Officer
J.P. Goebbels	1897	Lower class	PhD in Philology; Journalist
H. Göring	1893	Minor gentry (elite)	Air ace in WW I
R. Hess	1894	Elite	W. Front, served in Hitler's regiment; *Freikorps*
H. Himmler	1900	Lower middle class	Lab. technician; chicken farmer
A. Hitler	1887	Lower middle class	W. Front; political agitator
E. Röhm	1887	Lower middle class	W. Front; joined *Reichswehr*
A. Rosenberg	1893	Lower middle class	Served in Russian army (Estonian); journalist
G. Strasser	1892	Lower middle class	W. Front; owned chemist's shop

Based on information from J. Taylor and W. Shaw, *A Dictionary of the Third Reich*, 1987

2.17   A social analysis of Nazi party membership

Table 1 is an analysis of the gainfully employed population of Germany by occupations and classes in 1933. The lower class includes both skilled and unskilled manual workers; the lower middle class (*unterer Mittelstand*) incorporates minor civil servants, so that Hitler's father would have belonged to it. The elite also includes the old Junker aristocracy as well as the professionals and managers   5
mentioned here. Table 4 analyses the membership of the Nazi party in nine different areas at different times, in terms of the social categories listed in Table 1.

Barmen (B), Langerfeld (C), Mülheim (D) and Mettmann (F) are in the Ruhr; Brunswick (E), Hamburg (A), Königsberg city (H) and Königsberg city and surroundings (I) are in the North; Starnberg (G) is in Bavaria. The term   10
'frequency' simply indicates the total number of members in each area.

1 *Frequencies and percentages of occupations and classes in gainfully employed German population, Reich, summer 1933*

Class	Occupational subgroup	Frequency	Per cent of total
Lower	1 Unskilled workers	10,075,782	37.25
	2 Skilled (craft) workers	4,478,803	16.56
	3 Other skilled workers	203,737	0.75
Subtotal		14,758,322	54.56
Lower middle	4 Master craftsmen (independent)	2,585,551	9.56
	5 Non-academic professionals	483,208	1.79
	6 Lower and intermediate (petty) employees	3,359,248	12.42
	7 Lower and intermediate (petty) civil servants	1,402,189	5.18
	8 Merchants (self-employed)	1,624,118	6.00
	9 Farmers (self-employed)	2,082,912	7.70
Subtotal		11,537,226	42.65
Elite	10 Managers	143,659	0.53
	11 Higher civil servants	128,794	0.48
	12 Academic professionals	259,310	0.96
	13 Students (university and upper school)	129,292	0.48
	14 Entrepreneurs	91,296	0.34
Subtotal		752,351	2.78
Total		27,047,899	100.00

Both tables are taken from Michael Kater, *The Nazi Party, A Social Profile of Members and Leaders, 1919–1945*, 1983, pp. 241, 246

4 *Percentages of members of NSDAP chapters by social class and occupational subgroup in various German towns, 1925–29*

Class	Occupational subgroup	(A) Hamburg Mar. 1925	(B) Barmen [Apr. 1925]	(C) Langerfeld Nov. 1925	(D) Mülheim Nov. 1925	(E) Brunswick 1925–26	(F) Mettmann Feb. 1926	(G) Starnberg July 1927	(H) Königsberg [1928]	(I) Königsberg Jun. 1929
Lower	1 Unskilled workers	17.9	10.7	27.0	15.6	13.3	28.6	14.8	5.6	2.5
	2 Skilled (craft) workers	13.8	28.7	27.0	28.9	13.9	14.3	21.1	22.7	21.4
	3 Other skilled workers	1.9	4.9	2.7	6.7	2.3	3.6	11.1	4.7	3.8
Subtotal		33.6	44.3	56.8	51.1	29.5	46.4	47.0	33.0	27.7
Lower middle	4 Master craftsmen	7.9	16.4	16.2	15.6	8.0	7.1	12.2	13.1	12.4
	5 Non-academic professionals	0	0.8	2.7	2.2	2.3	0	0	3.9	1.7
	6 Lower employees	14.2	17.2	0	17.8	19.5	32.1	7.4	14.2	20.0
	7 Lower civil servants	8.5	2.5	5.4	2.2	11.7	7.1	11.1	5.6	6.7
	8 Merchants	30.2	17.2	13.5	11.1	15.6	0	0	14.2	18.3
	9 Farmers	0	0.8	0	0	7.8	3.6	0	4.3	0.8
Subtotal		60.8	54.9	37.8	48.9	64.9	50.0	30.7	55.3	59.9
Elite	10 Managers	0.9	0	0	0	1.6	0	0	0	0.4
	11 Higher civil servants	0.9	0	0	0	0	0	14.8	0.9	0.8
	12 Academic professionals	3.8	0	2.7	0	2.3	0	3.7	1.3	2.1
	13 Students	0	0.8	2.7	0	0.8	3.6	0	7.8	7.9
	14 Entrepreneurs	0	0	0	0	0.8	0	3.7	1.7	1.3
Subtotal		5.6	0.8	5.4	0	5.5	3.6	22.2	11.7	12.5
Per cent total		100	100	100	100	100	100	100	100	100
Frequency		106	122	37	45	128	28	27	232	240

Theodore Abel's enquiry elicited 680 replies, and formed the basis of a book entitled *Why Hitler Came into Power*, published in 1938. The following excerpts have been selected to indicate the social range of Nazi supporters in the early days of the party, and their reasons for joining it.

2.18 Individual case histories

(a) A petty tradesman

I moved to Shoenbeck where unemployment forced me on the dole. On these beggarly alms my wife and I managed to subsist until 1927. From that time until 1929 I made a living as a pedlar. When we consider that on the one hand the policies of the Red government, particularly the inflation and taxes, deprived me of   5
all means of livelihood, while on the other hand we soldiers of the front line were being ruled by a gang of exploiters ready to stoop to any means to seize the starvation wages of our suffering, duped comrades, it will become clear why a number of us welcomed the activities of patriotic groups, particularly those of the Hitler movement.   10

(b) A physician

I first heard of the National Socialist party in 1928. I became interested, and attended a meeting. There one Dr. Ley gave a remarkable analysis of governmental responsibility for the plight of Germany, at the same time outlining the aims and purposes of National Socialism. The speaker's ideas were so thoroughly after my   15
own heart, that he seemed, in fact, to be expressing my own thoughts and desires. I was swept off my feet, and I made up my mind to join the party without delay.

(c) A railway worker

As a railroad worker, I had ample opportunity to observe the prevalent confusion, particularly among workers. While I was in the army, I found that the best soldiers   20
came from the working class; now I had to witness these workers being alienated from the Fatherland. Why then should Germany rend itself? I shuddered at the thought of Germany in the grip of Bolshevism. The slogan 'Workers of the world unite!' made no sense to me. At the same time, however, National Socialism, with its promise of a community of blood, barring all class struggle, attracted me   25
profoundly.

(d) A farmer

At Easter 1926 I left the gymnasium and went home to the farm. Here Dame Care was our guest. Scarcity of funds necessitated borrowing at usurious rates of interest. Since the loans could not be paid back the day they were due, they were added to   30
the debts, so that these grew unbearable in a short time . . . Always the Jew was the obligingly smiling money-lender and devilishly grinning collector of debts. Thus it

went on until 1931 . . . In March 1931, after a short quarrel with my father, I left my home and went out into the world . . . if up to now I had been a National Socialist from the farmer's point of view, I now had the best opportunity to study   35
the labourer's problem. In doing this, one thing became clear to me. The class prejudices of those in higher positions must first disappear before the back of the class struggle can be broken . . . National Socialism had become my inner conviction.

Motives for joining   40

(e) The fact is, Hitler looks every man in the eye. His looks wander from one trooper to another as the *SA* marches by. We, old-time National Socialists, did not join the *SA* for reasons of self-interest. Our feelings led us to Hitler. There was a tremendous surge in our hearts, a something that said: 'Hitler you are our man. You speak as a soldier of the front and as a man; you know the grind, you yourself have   45
been a working man. You have lain in the mud, even as we – no big shot, but an unknown soldier. You have given your whole being, all your warm heart, to German manhood, for the well-being of Germany rather than your personal advancement or self-seeking. For your innermost heart will not let you do otherwise.
(f) Seldom was our people united and great. But whenever it was strongly unified,   50
it was unconquerable. This then is the secret of our idea, and in it lies the power of National Socialism: Unity is the goal of our leader, who wants to make the people strong, so it may become powerful again.
(g) As a result of the lessons of history and my own experience both during and after the war, I became a nationalist. The suffering and privations of wide strata of   55
our people, on the other hand, made me a socialist.

In 1925 the Army of Occupation lifted the ban against the National Socialist party in my home town. I attended the initial meetings, and found that the Party subscribed to the very aims and purposes I cherished. I joined the movement, and have been one of its active workers ever since.   60

(Sixty per cent of the contributors make no reference whatsoever to indicate that they harboured anti-Semitic feelings.)
(h) i After the assassination of Rathenau I began a searching inquiry into the Jewish question. I read a great deal, and it became increasingly clear to me that international Marxism and the Jewish problem are closely bound together. In this   65
fact I recognise the cause of the political, moral and cultural decay of my Fatherland. I studied the solutions proposed by the various parties, and I convinced myself that the National Socialist programme is not only thoroughly justified but absolutely necessary for the rebirth of Germany.
(h) ii I was greatly impressed by the first meeting I attended. It quickened my   70
pulse to hear about the Fatherland, unity and the need for a supreme leader. I felt that I belonged to these people. Only their statements about the Jews I could not swallow. They gave me a headache even after I had joined the party.

Theodore Abel, *Why Hitler Came to Power***, 1978**

Questions

1 What characteristics were shared by those who were Nazi leaders in 1928 [2.16]?

2 How far do Tables 1 and 4 [2.17] support the view that, in relation to the overall composition of Germany's class structure, the lower middle class was over-represented and the lower class under-represented in the Nazi party between 1924 and 1929?

3 Over the same period, in relation to their share of total employment, which occupational groups provided a more than proportionate percentage of Nazi party members [2.17]?

4 What reasons can you give for the discrepancies between different areas in the percentages of Nazi party members belonging to each social group [Table 4, 2.17]?

5 Do you think that the statistical evidence presented in Table 4 [2.17] is sufficient to justify firm conclusions about the social composition of the Nazi party?

6 Analyse the different motives for joining the Nazi party in 2.18(f–h) and relate them to the individual histories given in 2.18(a–e).

7 What evidence of genuine idealism among Nazi party supporters can you find in 2.18?

3 The collapse of the Weimar Republic and Hitler's accession to the Chancellorship

The two processes described in this chapter are closely related, but Hitler's rise to power was not the necessary consequence of the collapse of the Weimar Republic. Up to the final moment when he became Chancellor the outcome was still in doubt, and there remain a number of tantalising moments at which history might have taken a different course. Nor was the fate of the Weimar Republic preordained. Under President Ebert the twin crises of inflation and the French occupation of the Ruhr were successfully weathered. Between 1924 and 1928 Germany enjoyed relative prosperity and internal peace. In 1926 German entry into the League of Nations marked her return to international respectability. Yet by July 1932 the Nazi party was the largest in the *Reichstag* and by January 1933 Hitler was installed in the Chancellery.

It is the purpose of this chapter to explain this untoward, and to some extent unexpected, development. The first section explores both the strengths and weaknesses of the Weimar Republic in its years of prosperity; the second examines the impact on Germany of the economic crisis which enveloped both Europe and the United States between 1928 and 1932; the final section charts Hitler's route to power through the ballot box, and the conversion of right-wing forces to the prospects of a Nazi-based government which they thought they could control.

The strengths and weaknesses of the Weimar Republic, 1924–28

At the time of the Munich *putsch* in November 1923 Germany was experiencing savage inflation. The value of the mark fell from 76.7 to the dollar in July 1921, to 4,200,000,000,000 in November 1923. From January 1923 until August 1924 the Ruhr was occupied by French and Belgian troops. As if that were not enough, the Weimar government had to face the threat of Communist risings in Saxony and Thuringia, as well as a militant Bavarian separatist movement. Yet each challenge was met. Gustav Stresemann, leader of the *DVP*, who became Chancellor in August 1923, abandoned the policy of passive resistance to the occupation of the Ruhr, and this brought about French withdrawal. The currency was stabilised through the issue of a new *Renten-mark*, whose circulation was tightly controlled. The *Reichswehr* showed itself willing to combat opposition from the Right as well as the Left and Bavarian separatism was contained.

The Dawes Plan, which came into effect in August 1924, scaled down annual reparations payments to acceptable levels and initiated a loan to tide the German government over its immediate difficulties. During the next four years Germany received 25.5 billion marks in foreign loans and paid back 22.9 billion marks in reparations. The German economy responded to the more favourable international climate, and most economic indicators, if not all, showed an improvement [3.1(a–c)].

The wounds inflicted by the Treaty of Versailles also began to heal. Stresemann, who remained as Foreign Secretary after giving up the Chancellorship in November 1923, successfully negotiated the Locarno Pact with France and Britain, signed in December 1925. Under this agreement Germany accepted her western frontiers as final, and while Stresemann refused to make the same undertaking over her eastern boundaries, changes would be made by arbitration rather than the use of force. In March 1926 Germany entered the League of Nations and was given a seat on the Council. Stresemann gained two further concessions: under the Young Plan of 1929, annual reparations payments were again scaled down (though the repayment period was extended to sixty years); and France and Britain agreed to withdraw their forces from the Rhineland in 1930, five years earlier than the date stipulated in the Treaty of Versailles.

Against these indisputable gains there has to be set the evidence of disturbing faults in the economic and political structure of the Weimar Republic and the continuance of sharp political divisions. The economic indicators were not all favourable. Unemployment remained high; German industry was dangerously dependent on foreign investment; German agriculture suffered from falling prices and growing indebtedness. Political instability was an endemic problem. No party secured an overall majority in the *Reichstag* and there were no fewer than fifteen different cabinets between 1919 and 1928, none of which lasted longer than eighteen months. The moderate parties, committed to the working of parliamentary democracy, were plagued by internal divisions, while the extremist parties on the Left and the Right continued to attract a hard core of supporters even during the years of prosperity. The *Reichswehr* might have claimed to be above politics, but many of its senior officers opposed Stresemann's policies and covertly undermined the disarmament clauses of the Treaty of Versailles. 3.1–3.6 illustrate both these strengths and weaknesses.

The economy

3.1(a)   Index of industrial production (selected years)

(1928 = 100)

Year	Capital goods	Consumption goods	Total
1920	56	51	54
1921	65	69	54
1922	70	74	70
1923	43	57	46
1924	65	81	69
1925	80	85	81
1926	77	80	78
1927	97	103	98
1928	100	100	100
1929	102	97	100
1930	84	91	87
1931	62	82	70
1932	47	74	58

V.R. Berghahn, *Modern Germany*, 1982, p. 258

3.1(b)   Unemployment (annual averages)

Year	No. (000s)	% of working population
1921	346	1.8
1922	215	1.1
1923	818	4.1
1924	927	4.9
1925	682	3.4
1926	2025	10.0
1927	1312	6.2
1928	1391	6.3
1929	1899	8.5
1930	3076	14.0
1931	4520	21.9
1932	5603	29.9

V.R. Berghahn, *Modern Germany*, 1982, p. 266

3.1(c)   German agricultural debt, 1925–30 (m. Reichsmarks)

Year	Secured loans	Medium-term loans	Short-term credits	Total
1925	1 011.3	25.8	2 186.1	3 223.2
1926	2 048.5	101.8	2 127.0	4 277.3
1927	2 814.4	304.4	2 565.8	5 684.6
1928	3 623.3	318.0	2 889.8	6 831.1
1929	4 177.1	360.4	2 865.2	7 342.7
1930	4 373.0	330.2	3 088.1	7 791.3

Harold James, *The German Slump, Politics and Economics, 1924–1936*, 1986, p. 255

3.2   Recovery or Collapse: *A Report of the Reichsverband der Deutschen Industrie* (Association of German Industry), December 1929

The policies of recent years have been dominated by an 'immense disparity between productivity and profitability on the one hand and public spending on the other'. In 1924 Germany began with no investment capital, and the first task ought to have been building it, not attempting to create a welfare state. Too many compromises with socialism led to 'politically motivated interference in the economy'.   5

Public costs had skyrocketed: Not counting social insurance, 'public spending is more than triple the 1913 level', and taxes were up from 4 to 14 billion annually; social insurance costs had risen from 1.2 to 5.5 billion annually between 1913 and 1929, they claimed.

A 40 per cent increase in incomes in five years and luxurious consumption were   10 just not justifiable. 'With rising wages, rising taxes, rising interest rates and declining profits, the point is reached where maintaining production itself no longer makes sense . . . Only responsible economic policies can prevent the collapse of the economy and aid in making Germany free in foreign policy.'

D. Abraham, *The Collapse of the Weimar Republic*, new edition, 1986, p. 227

Questions

1 What do the figures in 3.1(a–c) indicate about the stability of the German economy under the Weimar Republic?
2 How would you explain the steady increase in farm indebtedness between 1925 and 1930? What were its political consequences?
3 What weaknesses in the German economy are identified in 3.2? Do you think a dispassionate observer would have agreed with this diagnosis?
4 Does the evidence presented in 3.1 and 3.2 suggest that without the Wall Street Crash Germany would have avoided a depression?

The political situation

3.3 Election Results, 1920–33 (main parties only)

Seats gained in the Reichstag

	6 June 1920	5 May 1924	7 Dec. 1924	20 May 1928
Communist (*KPD*)	4	62	99	54
Independent Socialist (*USPD*)	83			
Social Democrat (*SPD*)*	103	103	131	153
Centre*	64	65	69	61
Bavarian People's Party (*BVP*)*	21	16	19	17
German Democratic Party (*DDP*)*	39	28	32	25
German People's Party (*DVP*)*	65	45	51	45
German National Party (*DNVP*)	71	95	103	73
National Socialist (Nazi, *NSDAP*)		32	14	12

	14 Sept. 1930	31 July 1932	11 Nov. 1932	3 March 1933
Communist (*KPD*)	77	89	100	81
Independent Socialist (*USPD*)				
Social Democrat (*SPD*)*	143	133	121	120
Centre*	68	75	70	74
Bavarian People's Party (*BVP*)*	19	22	20	18
German Democratic Party (*DDP*)*	20	4	2	5
German People's Party (*DVP*)*	30	7	11	2
German National Party (*DNVP*)	41	37	52	52
National Socialist (Nazi, *NSDAP*)	107	230	196	288

Note: *Parties which supported the Weimar Republic

V.R. Berghahn, *Modern Germany*, 1982, p. 284 (adapted)

Questions

1 Which parties attracted the most consistent levels of support between 1920 and 1933?
2 How do you account for this?
3 Which parties experienced greatest losses between 1928 and 1933?
4 Would it be reasonable to infer from these figures that the Nazi party made its main gains during these five years from among the Protestant middle class?

Germany's international position

Attitudes to the Treaties of Locarno

In the debate on the Locarno Treaties in the *Reichstag* (1925), the party executive of the *DNVP* (the German National People's Party) voted to withdraw their ministers from the cabinet and instructed the *Reichstag* members to vote against the treaty. Chancellor Hans Luther, who belonged to the *DVP*, protested as follows to Count Westarp (leader of the *DNVP*):

3.4(a)

We have achieved one hundred per cent of what we undertook to achieve at Locarno! Never has a delegation had such a success! We were a people of helots, and today we are once more a state of world consequence! A storm of resentment will sweep the German Nationalist party away if it mutilates this achievement!

G.A. Craig, *Germany, 1866–1945*, 1978, p. 519

In April 1926 General von Seekt, Chief of the Army Command from March 1920 to October 1926, wrote to his sister:

3.4(b)

The situation has deteriorated considerably since last year. In foreign affairs I consider the Locarno–Geneva policy wrong because it ties us and brings no advantage. We are still too weak to give any direction, and are thus always led by others, never leading, at most a compliant ally whom one can drop when one gets reconciled or can find a better one. We could have waited and become internally   5
stronger first, above all we could have kept an entirely free hand towards the East. This we no longer have. We have succumbed to British influence and are serving British interests. Our representatives are, after all, little men who are no match for British diplomacy and its kind condescension, like the chancellor, and ambitious busy-bodies who must have their finger in every pie, like Stresemann, the man of   10
general distrust; but it seems impossible to get rid of him . . .

F.L. Carsten, *The Reichswehr and Politics, 1918–1933*, 1966, pp. 207–8

Here is the view of a German journalist, Victor Schiff, who had been present at the signing of the Treaty of Versailles, writing from the standpoint of 1929:

3.4(c)

And yet! In comparison with what we expected after Versailles, Germany has raised herself up to shoulder the terrific burden of this peace in a way we should never have thought possible. So that today after ten years, we may say with certainty as we take a look at the opinions and prophesies of the time: 'Even so, it might have been worse.' Those must admit it who held that to reject the Treaty would be the lesser   5
of two evils. Nobody can prove that those 'nos' of 1919 were wrong, but at least it is incontestable that the 'ayes' in Weimar were justified historically . . .

And this at least may be said with assurance. In spite of every set-back, which alas, we shall have to experience, since here and abroad the forces of nationalism are strong enough to play into each other's hands – the spirit of Versailles has been   10
conquered . . . The stages of convalescence from Versailles were: Spa, Genoa, London, Locarno, Geneva. From the Versailles palisades to the welcome and friendly banquet at Geneva is a very long road indeed to go, and we have travelled it surprisingly quickly.

V. Schiff, *The Germans at Versailles*, 1930, pp. 198–220

Attitudes to Disarmament and Reparations

3.5 'Guidelines on Military Policy', Proceedings of the Social Democratic Party Conference, 1929

To the German Republic has fallen the historic mission of leading the way to international disarmament. She cannot fulfil this mission if she violates her armaments limitations (even though these were unilaterally imposed) and if, by trying to evade or violate them, she gives other persons a reason or an excuse to renounce international disarmament agreements and build up even stronger   5
armaments.

R.N. Hunt, *German Social Democracy*, 1964, p. 37

In the same year, 1929, Alfred Hugenberg, who had replaced Count Westarp as leader of the *DNVP* in October 1928, formed a committee (which included Hitler) to oppose the Young Plan. In September this committee produced a draft law which attracted 4,135,000 signatures, enough to have it debated in the *Reichstag*, where it secured 55 votes. It was also the subject of a referendum in December 1929, when it won 5,825,000 votes, well short of the 21 million needed to secure its passage, but still an indication of the significant opposition to the spirit of Locarno.

3.6(a)   Terms of the referendum on the Young Plan

1 The Reich Government will solemnly inform the foreign powers without delay that the compulsory recognition of war guilt in the Versailles Treaty contradicts historical truth, is based on false preconceptions, and is not binding in international law.

3 New burdens and obligations *vis-à-vis* foreign powers on the basis of the recognition of war guilt may not be undertaken. This also includes the burdens and obligations which are to be undertaken by Germany on the basis of the Paris experts and the agreements deriving therefrom [i.e. the Young Plan].

Nazism, 1919–1945, ed. J. Noakes and G. Pridham, vol. I, 1983, pp. 64–5

3.6(b)   Poster advertising a meeting for opponents to the Young Plan

Volksversammlung

gegen den

Youngplan

am 26. September 1929, abends 8 Uhr
Aula der Herderschule, Charlottenburg, Westend: Bayern-Allee 2

60 Jahre jede Sekunde 80 Goldmark wollen wir nicht zahlen!

The text reads: 'People's meeting against the Young Plan . . . We do not want to pay 80 gold marks every second for 60 years!'

Bundesarchiv Koblenz

Questions

1 Summarise and distinguish between the respective views of the Treaties of Locarno advanced in 3.4(a) and 3.4(b).
2 How reliable a guide to the real sentiments of the author is each source?
3 Explain the references to Spa, Genoa, London, Locarno and Geneva in 3.4(c).
4 What is meant by the phrase 'the spirit of Versailles has been conquered' [3.4(c), lines 10–11]?
5 From the evidence presented in 3.4–3.6, would it be fair to say that a majority of Germans accepted the Treaty of Versailles as the price to pay for Germany's re-admission to the international community on equal terms?
6 Did the terms of the Treaty of Versailles mean that the *SPD*'s policy on disarmament [3.5] was doomed from the outset?
7 How serious was German opposition to the Young Plan?

Weimar governments and the economic crisis, 1928–32

The German economy was already showing signs of strain in 1928. Investment had begun to fall and unemployment to rise well before the Wall Street Crash in October 1929. But the withdrawal of American loans, particularly after the banking crisis of 1931, and the loss of export markets that accompanied the great depression made a serious situation very much worse. Unemployment in Germany climbed inexorably as industrial production fell, reaching a record total of over 5.6 million in 1932. Against this backcloth were played out the political manoeuvres that led to the final demise of the Republic.

So far as the government was concerned, the most serious symptom of the crisis was the growing budget deficit caused by a fall in tax receipts and increases in welfare payments to the unemployed. It was primarily the failure of successive cabinets to find acceptable solutions to this problem that led to the assumption of dictatorial powers by the Brüning government. More generally, the failure to halt the rise in unemployment led to disillusion with parliamentary democracy and growing support for the alternatives offered by the Communists and the Nazis.

The election of May 1928 produced to all appearances the most hopeful result achieved under the Weimar Republic [3.3]. The *SPD* gained 22 seats; the *DNVP*, the *NASDP* and the *KPD* all lost ground. More significantly, the *SPD* agreed to join a Great Coalition of the moderate parties for the first time since 1920, under the leadership of Hermann Müller. But almost from the start Müller's government ran into difficulties. True to their pacifist inclinations, the

SPD delegation in the Reichstag voted against the building of the first armoured cruiser permitted under the Treaty of Versailles. Hugenberg and his allies led a vociferous campaign against the Young Plan. By the winter of 1929 it was clear that the government's finances were running into deficit. The DVP was unwilling to accept any increases in taxation, while the SPD was opposed to any increases in insurance contributions or cuts in unemployment benefit.

The crisis came to a head in March 1930. The SPD refused to accept a compromise proposal put forward by Brüning (Centre party) and Mayer (DDP) under which welfare payments would continue to be subsidised out of taxation up to a certain limit, but would thereafter be met by an increase in employers' and employees' contributions from 3.5 to 3.75 per cent of wages and salaries. Unable to secure a majority for this proposal, the Müller cabinet resigned en bloc on 27 March. On 30 March Hindenburg sent for Heinrich Brüning, leader of the Centre, to form the next government. Brüning was determined to follow a policy of rigid financial orthodoxy, increasing taxes and cutting public spending until the budget was balanced. Unfortunately one of his first proposals, a $2\frac{1}{2}$ per cent tax on the salaries of government officials, was defeated in the Reichstag by 256 votes to 193. Brüning, with Hindenburg's approval, decided to invoke Article 48 (see 1.6) and put through the tax changes by presidential decree. An SPD motion condemning the decrees was passed by 236 votes to 221. This procedure was also authorised, under section 3 of Article 48. Brüning broke the constitutional impasse by securing the dissolution of the Reichstag, 'one of the most fateful events in the history of the Weimar Republic' (E. Eyck, The History of the Weimar Republic, vol. II, 1967). The first of a series of deflationary measures was implemented by presidential decree on 26 July, to be followed by a further five over the next eighteen months. Their combined impact was considerable. Insurance contributions were raised to $6\frac{1}{2}$%. Civil service pay fell by 23% overall; the beer duty was raised by 50%. Unemployment benefit was cut by 5%. In December 1931 wages were reduced to their January 1926 levels, in defiance of existing collective agreements. By the end of 1931 government expenditure had fallen from 13.1 billion marks to 11.3 billion, a drop of 13% in current prices, 9.8% in real terms. The fall in purchasing power exacerbated unemployment, and while schemes for spending on public works (roads, flood protection and land reclamation) were considered as a remedy, no financial provision was made to implement them.

Economists and historians have long debated whether there were realistic alternatives to Brüning's policies. 3.7 and 3.8 indicate the views of some of his contemporaries. 3.7 is an excerpt from a speech by Fritz Tarnow, trade unionist, member of the SPD, and Chairman of the Woodworkers' Union, during proceedings of the Allgemeiner Deutscher Gewerkschaftsbund (Federation of Socialist Trade Unions, *ADGB*) in 1931. In 3.8, R.J. Overy, a British economic historian, summarises possible alternatives to Brüning's policies.

3.7

Are we sitting at the sick-bed of capitalism, not only as doctors who want to cure the patient, but also as cheerful heirs who cannot wait for the end and would like to hasten it with poison? Our entire situation is expressed in this image. We are condemned, I think, to be doctors who seriously desire and care, and yet we also maintain the feeling that we are heirs who wish to receive the entire legacy of the   5
capitalist system today rather than tomorrow. This double role, doctor and heir, is a damned difficult task.

R.N. Hunt, *German Social Democracy*, 1964, pp. 38–9

3.8

Chancellor Brüning appears as the typical pre-Keynesian politician. Yet this was not the case. There were alternative economic strategies available and some were widely canvassed at the time. Throughout 1931 and 1932 an active debate was carried over the appropriate economic strategy for Germany to adopt. Opposed to the orthodox laissez-faire economists were those like Wilhelm Ropke, whose reports for the   5
Brauns-Commission [a Commission of experts set up by Brüning in 1931] stressed the need for a 'first spark' (*Initialzündung*) in the form of government investment programmes to get industrial production going again. . . Books like those by Drager on *Arbeitbeschaffung durch Kreditschöpfung* ('Work-creation through the productive creation of credit') and Wagemann on *Geld- und Kreditreform* (Money and Credit   10
Reform), both published in 1932, could have provided the government with a theoretical basis for expansionary policies . . . The problem faced by those favouring unorthodox expansionary policies was their lack of political influence. This was not just because Brüning himself now seems to have been opposed to schemes of deficit-financing on theoretical grounds, but to the fact that champions of a new economic   15
theory were of junior rank or were outsiders like Ropke [a university professor] or Woytinska [economic adviser to the *ADGB*] with no political power base.

R.J. Overy, *The Nazi Economic Recovery, 1932–1938*, 1982, p. 24

Questions

1 What did Fritz Tarnow mean by saying that he and his fellow trade unionists were both 'doctors' and 'heirs' at the sick-bed of capitalism [3.7]?
2 What particular dilemma faced the Social Democrats when they were confronted with Brüning's economic policies?
3 What 'alternative economic strategies' [3.8] for dealing with unemployment were there between 1930 and 1932, and why were they not pursued?

The fall of the Brüning government

Faced with a parallel situation in Britain, Ramsay MacDonald's minority Labour government pursued policies very similar to Brüning's. But when MacDonald's cabinet split on the issue of cuts in unemployment benefit the ensuing crisis was resolved by the formation of a National Government, which then won a massive endorsement for what were held to be its necessary though unpopular policies in the general election of 1931. Brüning was not so fortunate. In September 1930 he put his policies to the test in a general election with disastrous results [3.3, 3.9]. The Centre party retained its share of the vote, but the other moderate parties, the *DDP* and the *DVP*, lost much support. The Communists gained 23 seats and the National Socialist representation leapt from 12 to 107. Lacking a popular mandate, Brüning had to rely on the tolerance of the *SPD* and the continuing support of Hindenburg.

The worsening employment situation and the suspension of parliamentary government led to an escalation of political violence, mainly in the form of street clashes between the *SA* and the Communists. In April 1932, not before time, General Groener, now Minister of Defence and Minister of the Interior, urged the banning of the *SA* [3.10]. On 13 April Hindenburg signed a decree to that effect. But he very soon had second thoughts. Many right-wing forces, including one of the Kaiser's sons, supported the *SA* [3.11]. Groener survived a vote of confidence in the *Reichstag* by 287 votes to 257, but nevertheless felt he must resign from his position as Minister of Defence on 13 May. Hindenburg disliked what he took to be Brüning's subservience to the *SPD*, and he also entertained exaggerated fears that indebted estates in East Prussia were about to be redistributed to poor farmers. On 29 May he informed Brüning that he would no longer support his government. Brüning resigned the following day. His fall owed more to right-wing prejudice than to the unpopularity of his economic policies. **3.9–3.11** relate to these events.

3.9   Brüning's decision to hold an election

The election became a plebiscite on the emergency decrees, but at the same time a fight for decision between a senseless form of parliamentarism and a sound and judicious democracy, in which the government, in order to save public finances from collapse, had to take up the struggle for this objective before the whole people in face of the intriguing and the foolishness of the existing Reichstag.

Heinrich Brüning, *Memoiren*, cited in G.A. Craig, *Germany, 1866–1945*, 1978, p. 540

3.10 Groener's decision to ban the *SA*, letter to Brüning, 10 April 1932

It is not consistent with the sovereignty of the state that a political party be permitted to maintain a private army organised in a military fashion, the leaders of which – generally from army officers – necessarily bring it into conflict with the police and the organs of the state through their effort to develop the military effectiveness of their forces for promoting their special interests.

E. Eyck, *A History of the Weimar Republic*, vol. II, 1967, p. 360

3.11 Letter to Groener from Crown Prince Frederick William (one of Kaiser William II's sons), 14 April, 1932

I find it incomprehensible that precisely you, as a minister of defence, wish to help disperse the wonderful human resources which are united in the *SA* and the *SS*, and which are receiving such valuable training there . . . The dissolution of the *SA* and *SS* must shatter the confidence of the national circles in the ministry of defence.

F.L. Carsten, *The Reichswehr and Politics, 1918–1933*, 1966, pp. 344–5

Questions

1 How would Brüning have distinguished between 'a senseless form of parliamentarism' and 'a sound and judicious democracy' [3.9]?
2 Why did the Weimar governments tolerate the *SA* for so long and why was Groener's banning of it opposed in some right-wing circles [3.10, 3.11]?
3 'The dagger thrust with which he [Hindenburg] felled Brüning on May 30 in an unexampled display of infidelity, murdered not only the German Republic, but also the peace of Europe' (E. Eyck). Was Eyck being wise after the event when he made this judgement? Explain your answer.

The road to power, May 1932–January 1933

In Brüning's place, Hindenburg appointed Fritz von Papen, also nominally a member of the Centre party, but more importantly from Hindenburg's point of view a member of the German aristocracy and strongly conservative in his inclinations. Papen had no scruples about governing without a majority in the *Reichstag* but he was still anxious to put together a right-wing coalition. He could count on the backing of the *DNVP* under Hugenberg and he made a bid for Nazi support, seeing Hitler for the first time on 9 June. Two important consequences followed. The ban on the *SA* and the *SS* was lifted, and the *Reichstag* was dissolved in preparation for a general election to be held on 31 July. On 20 July Papen showed his true colours when he dissolved the

Social Democratic government in Prussia, taking personal control over the administration.

The election was preceded by a wave of violence in which the *SA* played a notable part. Ninety-nine people were killed and 1,125 were reported wounded. In Hamburg on Sunday 17 July there were at least thirteen deaths. What influence these events had on the outcome of the election is hard to say, but they certainly did no harm to the Nazi party, whose share of the vote, the highest recorded in a free election, reached 37.33 per cent, entitling the party to 230 seats in the *Reichstag*. Papen, like Brüning, had badly miscalculated. The Communists also raised their share of the vote to 14.3 per cent, giving them 89 seats. For the first time since the inauguration of the Weimar Republic the two extremist parties commanded a majority of seats in the *Reichstag*.

From the twelve seats it held in 1928 the Nazi party in the space of four years had become the largest in the *Reichstag*. How had it achieved this success? Historians are still seeking answers to this question. 3.12 (a, b) analyse the geographical distribution of Nazi votes and the changes in support for the Nazi party. 3.13–3.15 suggest some of the possible explanations for Nazi electoral gains.

3.12(a)   Votes cast for the Nazi party, 31 July 1932: geographical distribution

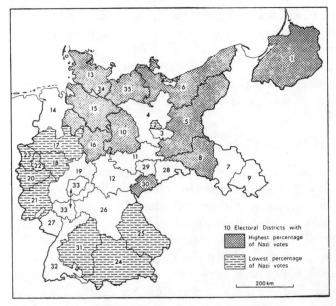

Nazism, 1919–1945, ed. J. Noakes and G. Pridham, vol. I, 1983, p. 82

3.12(b) Percentage of votes cast in favour of the *NSDAP*

Reichstag elections	4.v.24	7.xii.24	20.v.28	14.ix.30	31.vii.32	6.xi.32	5.iii.33
Number of seats	32	14	12	107	230	196	288
National vote (%)	6.5	3.0	2.6	18.3	37.3	33.1	43.9
Selected districts							
1 E. Prussia	8.6	6.2	0.8	22.5	47.1	39.7	56.5
2 Berlin	3.6	1.6	1.4	12.8	24.6	22.5	31.3
6 Pomerania	7.3	4.2	1.5	24.3	48.0	43.1	56.3
13 Schleswig-Holstein	7.4	2.7	4.0	27.0	51.0	45.76	53.2
17 Westphalia-North	3.5	1.3	1.0	12.2	25.7	22.3	34.9
20 Cologne-Aachen	1.5	0.6	1.1	14.5	20.2	17.4	30.1
22 Düsseldorf-East	3.9	1.6	1.8	17.0	31.6	27.0	37.4
24 Upper Bavaria	17.0	4.8	6.2	16.3	27.1	24.6	40.9
25 Lower Bavaria	10.2	3.0	3.5	12.0	20.4	18.5	39.2
27 Franconia	20.7	7.5	8.1	20.5	39.9	36.4	45.7
35 Mecklenburg	20.8	11.9	2.0	20.1	44.8	37.0	48.0

Note: Numbers in the left-hand margin correspond to the numbers in the map in 3.12(a).

Nazism, 1919–1945, ed. J. Noakes and G. Pridham, vol. I, 1983, p. 83

3.13   The diary of Frau Luise Solmitz, a Hamburg schoolteacher married to a former army officer, 1 June 1932

. . . I myself know that not only the desperate but those who purposely contract debts in our neighbourhood are enthusiastic Hitler people – as are all those who hope for something from a swing to the Left or the Right or anywhere. Nevertheless, every person who thinks and feels as a German, the bourgeois, the farmer, the aristocrat, the prince, and the intelligentsia, stands by Hitler. It is the   5
nationalist movement.

Nazism, 1919–1945, ed. J. Noakes and G. Pridham, vol. I, 1983, pp. 80–81

3.14   An explanation of middle and upper class support for Hitler

The National Socialists, as is well known, did not fully succeed in becoming a mass movement until Brüning became Chancellor and he consciously carried on the governmental practice of the imperial bureaucracy. But it was precisely the experience of the first presidential government of the Weimar republic which made it clear that a simple return to the pre-parliamentary division of power between   5
Reichstag and executive was no longer possible. A cabinet which governed in opposition to society was still less in a position to take the wind out of the sails of an anti-parliamentary mass movement than a weak parliamentary government could have done.

No schematic restoration of the pre-republican regime could, therefore, be the   10
right answer to the crisis of the Weimar system, but only a popular anti-parliamentarianism. If one was successfully to declare war on democracy, then it could only be done 'in the name of the people'. The only possible alternative to parliamentary democracy was the rule of the charismatic leader, legitimised by plebiscite . . .   15

If the cause of the success of the *NSDAP* among the middle classes is to be put in a nutshell then it was the combination of two promises which proved to be decisive: the National Socialists agreed in principle to maintain the traditional system of property relations and at the same time promised to radically liquidate the political system which no longer guaranteed the preservation of this order.   20

The majority of those who brought the National Socialists to power, either by giving them their votes or their money, wanted something different from that which became reality in the Third Reich. Both the middle and upper classes assumed that National Socialists wished to restore and modernise the political substance of the pre-republican system . . . In other words the supporters of the National Socialists   25
expected the destruction of the Marxist labour movement and the 'party state'; they hoped for a rigid authoritarian regime, which would cease to tolerate class struggles and ideological conflict. But so far as the National Socialist leadership was concerned, these were not the aims but merely essential prerequisites for the realisation of their aims. Hitler's long-term aspirations could not be diverted in   30
accordance with the economic needs of any social group; neither the fight against

the Jews, nor the essentially unlimited conquest of 'Lebensraum' sprang from a
concrete pressure of interests . . .

It may very well be that the Weimar Republic could have survived for a long
time had there not been the economic crisis of 1929. But it is just as likely that   35
German democracy could have survived without the authoritarian legacy of the
past.

H.A. Winkler, 'German Society and the Illusion of Restoration', *Journal of
Contemporary History*, October 1976, pp. 4–12

3.15   The widespread, if temporary, appeal of Nazism

The nucleus of the *NSDAP*'s following was formed by the small farmers,
shopkeepers and independent artisans of the old middle class, who constituted the
most stable, consistent component of the National Socialist constituency between
1924 and 1932. It was among these groups that the fear of social and economic
displacement associated with the emergence of modern industrial society was most   5
pronounced, and it was among these groups that the *NSDAP*'s corporatist, anti-
Marxist, anti-capitalist slogans struck their most responsive chord.

By 1932 the party had won considerable support among the upper middle class
student bodies of the universities, among civil servants, even in the middle and
upper grades and in the affluent electoral districts of Berlin, Hamburg and other   10
cities. Motivation was myriad, including fear of the Marxist left, frustrated career
ambitions, and resentment of the erosion of social prestige and security. Yet, while
sizeable elements of these groups undoubtedly felt their positions and prospects
threatened during the Weimar era, they cannot be described as uneducated,
economically devastated, or socially marginal. They belonged, in fact, to the   15
established elites of German society.

Just as the Nazis were winning support from elements of both upper and lower
middle classes, they also secured a significant constituency within the blue-collar
working class. Usually ignored or dismissed as unimportant, the *NSDAP*'s
prominent solicitation of a working class following and its success in the endeavour,   20
were exceptional in the context of German electoral politics.

By 1932 the *NSDAP* could, therefore, approach the German electorate claiming
the mantle of a coveted *Volkspartei*.

Yet, even at the height of its popularity at the polls, the *NSDAP*'s position as a
people's party was tenuous at best. If the party's support was a mile wide, it was at   25
critical points an inch deep. The *NSDAP* had managed to build a remarkably
diverse constituency, overcoming regional divisions, linking town and country,
spanning the social divides, and shrinking the gap between confessions. Yet, the
basis of that extraordinary electoral alliance was dissatisfaction, resentment and fear.
It therefore remains one of history's most tragic ironies that at precisely the moment   30
when the movement's electoral support had begun to falter, Hitler was installed as
Chancellor by representatives of those traditional elites who had done so much to

undermine the parliamentary system in Germany and who still believed that the National Socialist movement could be safely harnessed for their reactionary objectives.

T. Childers, *The Nazi Voter, the Social Foundations of Fascism in Germany, 1919–1933*, 1985, pp. 264–9

Questions

1 From the information given in 3.12(a, b) list in order the districts in which the Nazis did best and worst in the election of July 1932, and locate them on the map.

2 What explanations can you find for the disparities in regional support for Hitler (see 2.17 and 3.1(c))?

3 Why, according to H.A. Winkler, was Brüning's presidential style of government bound to fail [3.14]?

4 How far would you agree with Winkler's view that the German middle and upper classes voted for Hitler for reasons that had nothing to do with anti-Semitism or the demand for *Lebensraum*?

5 Compare the explanations given in 3.13, 3.14 and 3.15 for the increase in support for Nazism between 1930 and 1932. Do they differ significantly?

6 What does Childers mean when he writes [3.15, lines 25–6]: 'If the party's support was a mile wide, it was at critical points an inch deep'? What does this statement imply about the reasons for Hitler's rise to power?

7 Do 3.13–3.15 suggest that the Nazis had a different appeal for their hard-core members to that which they offered to the majority of voters who supported them in 1932? If so, what was the difference?

After the election result of July 1932 it might have been expected that Hitler would have been invited at least to participate in Papen's government. Two things prevented this outcome. Hitler refused to accept any post but the Chancellorship, and Hindenburg was unwilling to contemplate a government headed by Hitler, of whom he still held a low opinion. In the next few months a succession of events conspired to overcome Hindenburg's reluctance and to persuade Hitler to reduce his terms. Hitler improved his standing in right-wing circles, winning the support of men such as the industrialist Fritz von Thyssen, the banker Hjalmar Schacht and members of the *Reichslandbund*, an organisation which represented the interests of impoverished Prussian landowners. Secondly, the elections which Papen called in November 1932 produced a fall of 2 million votes for the Nazi party and a loss of 34 seats in the *Reichstag*. While this result still left the Nazis as the largest party, it convinced at least some of

Hitler's supporters that he should be prepared to consider entering a coalition government.

The election did nothing to strengthen Papen's position. Hitler still refused to join the cabinet except on his terms, and Papen's only suggestion, made to Hindenburg on 1 December, was that the *Reichstag* should go into recess and a constitutional reform bill be prepared. He did not specify its details. Schleicher, Minister of Defence, at this point informed Hindenburg that he could not answer for the *Reichswehr*'s ability to maintain law and order in view of the opposition Papen's scheme would undoubtedly arouse. Instead he suggested that he try to form a cabinet with the support of the trade unions and members of the Nazi party with socialist sympathies. Hindenburg preferred Schleicher's proposals to Papen's, and on 3 December Schleicher replaced Papen as Chancellor.

On the same day Schleicher had an interview with Gregor Strasser, who was offered the Vice Chancellorship. Strasser was inclined to accept, but when news of the offer reached Hitler he immediately summoned a meeting of Nazi leaders for 5 December, and followed this up with a meeting of the whole Nazi delegation on 7 December. Strasser was accused of attempting to split the party. Instead of rising to the challenge Strasser chose to resign from his position in the party (though not from the party itself) and departed to Italy on holiday. Schleicher's initiative never recovered from this rebuff.

The next three weeks were taken up with a complex series of meetings. It is hard to judge their importance, partly because the participants had such different recollections of what was decided at them. Among the most significant was a meeting held at the house of Baron Kurt von Schroeder in Cologne on 4 January between Papen and Hitler. What happened at that meeting is still a matter of controversy but at the very least Papen and Hitler had re-established contact. Another series of meetings with Papen began on 18 January, this time at the house of Joachim von Ribbentrop in the fashionable suburb of Dahlem, Berlin. Schleicher, in the meantime, failed to secure from Hindenburg the dissolution of the *Reichstag* and the proclamation of a state of emergency. On 28 January he resigned, and on Hindenburg's instructions Papen had another meeting with Hitler at which the terms on which Hitler would accept the Chancellorship were finally agreed. Hitler continued to step up his demands up to the moment of his appointment, securing Papen's agreement to an election only minutes before seeing Hindenburg to be sworn in. Hitler was to be one of only three Nazis in a cabinet of twelve. The others were Frick (Minister of the Interior) and Göring (Minister without Portfolio, Minister for Aviation and, crucially, Acting Minister for the Interior for Prussia). Papen wrote to a friend: 'I have got Hindenburg's confidence. In two months' time we will have squeezed Hitler into a corner until he squeaks' (*Aspects of the Third Reich*, ed. H.W. Koch, 1985, p. 511). Rarely can a prophecy have proved more mistaken.

Hitler's appointment as Chancellor finally depended on the overcoming of Hindenburg's opposition and the elimination of any other alternatives. 3.16–3.18 illustrate some of the reasons for this outcome.

3.16 A speech by Hitler to the Industry Club at Düsseldorf in January 1932, at Thyssen's invitation

People say to me so often: 'You are only the drummer of national Germany'. And suppose that I were only the drummer? It would today be a far more statesmanlike achievement to drum once more into this German people a new faith than gradually to squander the only faith they have . . . But we must first refashion the political pre-conditions: without that, industry and capacity, diligence and economy are in   5
the last resort of no avail; an oppressed nation will not be able to spend on its own welfare even the fruits of its own economy but must sacrifice them on the altar of exactions and of tribute. And so in contrast to our own official Government I see no hope for the resurrection of Germany if we regard the foreign politics of Germany as the primary factor: our primary need is the restoration of a sound national   10
German body politic, armed to strike. In order to realise this end I founded thirteen years ago the National Socialist movement: that movement I have led during the last twelve years and I hope that one day it will accomplish this task, and that, as the fairest result of its struggle, it will leave behind it a German body politic completely renewed internally, intolerant of anyone who sins against the nation and its   15
interests, intolerant of anyone who will not acknowledge its vital interests or who opposes them, intolerant and pitiless towards anyone who shall attempt once more to destroy or undermine this body politic, and yet ready for friendship and peace with anyone who has a wish for peace and friendship *(long and tumultuous applause)*.

The Speeches of Adolf Hitler, 1922–1939, ed. Norman H. Baynes, vol. I, 1942, pp. 826–9

3.17 Letter from Hjalmar Schacht to Hitler, 12 November 1932

Dear Herr Hitler:
Permit me to congratulate you on the firm stand you took after the election. I have no doubt that the present development of things can only lead to your becoming Chancellor. It seems as if our attempt to collect a number of signatures from business circles for this purpose was not altogether in vain, although I believe heavy   5
industry will hardly participate, for it rightfully bears its name 'heavy industry' on account of its indecisiveness.

I hope that in the next few days and weeks the slight difficulties which necessarily appear in the course of the propaganda campaign will not be so great as to provide the opponents with a reason for justified indignation: the stronger your internal   10 position is, the more dignified can be your fight. The more the cause develops in your favour, the more you can renounce personal attacks.

I am quite confident that the present system is certainly doomed to disintegration. With German Greetings,

Yours very truly,

(sgd) Hjalmar Schacht

15

R. Manvell and H. Fraenkel, *The Hundred Days to Hitler*, 1974, p. 103

3.18 Hitler becomes Chancellor

Left: Hitler, Vice Chancellor Papen and Blomberg (Minister for the *Reichswehr*), *Right:* the Field Marshall (Hindenburg) and the Corporal (Hitler) fight with us for Freedom and Equality.

Concentration Camp Dachau Catalogue, 1978, p. 30

Questions

1 What did Hitler mean by 'the restoration of a sound national German body politic, armed to strike' [3.16, lines 10–11]?

2 How far does the evidence presented in 3.16–3.17 support the view that German industry backed Hitler's bid for power?

3 What light does 3.18 throw on Hindenburg's readiness to appoint Hitler to the Chancellorship in 1933?

4 Did Hitler come to power by constitutional means? Justify your answer.

4 The Nazi regime at home

The making of a dictatorship

Papen's boast that Hitler would be boxed in by the Nationalist majority in the cabinet very quickly proved mistaken. In a rapid series of moves Hitler consolidated his own position, extended the authority of the Reich government over the individual German states and crushed all potential sources of opposition.

On 31 January 1933 in a broadcast to the German people Hitler explicitly condemned the shortcomings of the Weimar Republic and promised a complete break with the past [4.1]. On 27 February the destruction of the *Reichstag* by fire gave Hitler the opportunity to introduce an Emergency Decree under which all political rights guaranteed under the Weimar Constitution were temporarily suspended [4.2, 4.3]. In the elections held on 5 March the Nazi share of the vote rose to 43.9 per cent, giving the party 288 seats in the *Reichstag*, and, with the 52 seats gained by the Nationalists, an overall majority for the coalition. On 21 March Hitler attended a church service at the Nikolaikirche in the company of Hindenburg to mark a Day of National Awakening [4.4]. This was followed on 23 March by the passage of the Enabling Act [4.5(a, b)] in the *Reichstag* by 444 votes to 94, only the *SPD* voting against (though 81 Communist deputies would also have done so had they not been under arrest).

Laws for the Coordination of the States and the Reich introduced on 31 March and 7 April effectively emasculated elected governments in the states. On 2 May trade unions were banned, their offices raided and their leaders taken into 'protective custody'.

One by one the opposition parties were forced into dissolution. The Communist party was officially banned after 5 March. It had been allowed to contest the election simply to split the working-class vote. The *SPD* was outlawed on 22 June as 'hostile to the nation and the state'. The two moderate middle-class parties, the *DDP* and the *DVP*, already reduced to a tiny rump after the election of March 1933, voluntarily dissolved themselves on 28 June and 4 July respectively. The Catholic Centre party, which had participated in every one of the Weimar governments, was persuaded to vote itself out of existence on 5 July, largely, it would seem, on the strength of a Concordat with the Papacy, signed on 2 July, under which the church was guaranteed the right to maintain its own schools in return for an undertaking that its priests and organisations would abstain from political activities. The Nationalist party leader, Hugenberg, was dismissed from the cabinet on 27 June and the party dissolved itself at the same time. The undisputed authority of the Nazi party was finally confirmed by a law against the formation of new parties proclaimed on 14 July [4.6].

Before Hitler could feel totally secure he needed to assure himself that he had the support of the *Reichswehr*, and to overcome the threat to his authority posed by certain elements, notably Ernst Röhm, in the *SA*. He also needed to guard against any possibility of a right-wing move to restore the monarchy. In the summer of 1934 he disposed of both these dangers. Between 30 June and 3 July a bloodthirsty purge took place ('the night of the long knives') in which at least a hundred people were put to death, including Röhm, Gregor Strasser and General Schleicher. On the morning of 2 August, while Hindenburg was on his death-bed, the cabinet approved a law merging the offices of President and Chancellor [4.7]. This law was given retrospective validity by a plebiscite held on 18 August in which Hitler gained an overwhelming majority [4.8].

How had Hitler achieved such an astonishing triumph? Some have argued that 'the republic gave up' (H.W. Koch (ed.), *Aspects of the Third Reich*, p. 60); others maintain that even in 1933 the opposition was cowed by the use of violence, for instance in the March elections, and by intimidation [4.9]. A third possible explanation must surely lie in the sense of hope which Hitler was able to bring to the German people. His promises were believed, and on that premiss many Germans were prepared to give him the benefit of the doubt over episodes such as the July purge. 4.1–4.9 illustrate the transformation in Hitler's position between January 1933 and August 1934, and throw some light on the reasons for it.

4.1   Hitler's broadcast to the German People, 1 February 1933

More than fourteen years have passed since the unhappy day when, dazzled by promises from at home and abroad, the German people forgot its most precious possessions, our past, the Empire, its honour and freedom and thus lost everything. Since those days of betrayal the Almighty has withdrawn His blessing from our people. Discord and hatred came among us. With the deepest sorrow millions of the   5
best German men and women from all walks of life saw the unity of the nation

founder and disappear in a confusion of politically egotistical opinions, economic interests and opposing attitudes.

So the national government will regard it as its highest and first task to restore the united spirit and will of our people . . . It will take under its firm protection   10
Christianity, as the basis of our collective morality, and the family as the nurturer of our people and state. It will transcend position and class to bring our people again to an awareness of its national and political unity and the duties arising from this.

In fourteen years the November parties have ruined German farming. In fourteen years they have created an army of millions of unemployed. The national   15
government will carry out the following plan with iron resolution and the toughest persistence. Within four years the German farmer must be free from impoverishment. Within four years unemployment must be overcome permanently.

In foreign policy the national government will see its highest mission in the preservation of natural rights and thus in regaining the freedom of our people . . .   20
By its resolution to end the chaotic conditions in Germany it will help to introduce into the community of nations a state of equal worth and thus of course with equal rights. In doing this it is inspired by the greatness of the duty to support this free nation in maintaining and strengthening, as an equal, that peace which the world needs as never before. Now, German people, give us those four years and then   25
judge us and give your verdict!

Following the order of the Generalmarschall [Hindenburg] let us make a start. May Almighty God look graciously on our work, direct our purpose, bless our understanding and enrich us with the trust of our People. For we do not intend to fight for ourselves, but for Germany!

Max Domarus, *Hitler, Reden und Proklamationen, 1932–45*, vol. I, 1962, pp. 191–4, translated by M.J. Simpson

Questions

1 Explain the references to 'days of betrayal' in **4.1, line 4**.
2 Which 'fourteen years' is Hitler referring to in this passage **[line 1]**? Why does he give them such emphasis?
3 Comment on the tone of this broadcast. To which groups of Germans was it particularly intended to appeal?

The ending of individual rights to freedom of expression and association was effected by presidential decree on 28 February 1933 [**4.2**]. Hitler defended this action in an interview with a correspondent from the *Daily Express*, duly reported in the *Völkischer Beobachter* on 4 March [**4.3**].

4.2

Reich Law Gazette

1933	Published in Berlin, 28th February 1933

Decree of the Reich President on the protection of the people and the state, 28th February 1933.

On the basis of Article 48, para 2 of the constitution of the Reich the following is decreed as a protection against communist acts of violence endangering the state:

§1

Articles 114, 115, 117, 118, 123, 124 and 153 of the constitution of the German Reich are cancelled until further notice. This allows certain restrictions to be imposed on personal freedom, on the right to express a free opinion, the freedom of the press, of association and the right to hold meetings, it allows restrictions on the secrecy of the mail, post and telecommunications systems, the ordering of house searches and confiscation of property and restrictions on property rights.

§2

Should the necessary steps to restore public security and order not be taken in the Länder, the government of the Reich is empowered to enforce such measures in its capacity as the highest government authority.

§6

This decree applies from the day of publication.

Berlin, 28th February 1933.

Reich President
von Hindenburg

Reich Chancellor
Adolf Hitler

Interior Minister of the Reich
Frick

Justice Minister of the Reich
Dr. Gürtner

Questions on German History, 1984, p. 314

4.3

Europe ought to be grateful to me, instead of suspecting me of double dealing, for acting so firmly against the Bolsheviks. If Germany were to become Communist – which was a danger until I became Chancellor – it would not be long until the rest of Europe was in the grip of this Asiatic scourge. To the question whether the present suspension of civil liberties would continue, the Chancellor replied No! 5
Once the Communist threat is removed things will return to normal. Our laws were too liberal to enable me to deal appropriately and fast enough with the Underworld. But I myself am all too anxious for a normal situation to be restored as soon as possible. First, however, we must put an end to Communism.

Völkischer Beobachter, 4 March 1933, Microfilm MZ 9/22, *Institut für Zeitgeschichte*, Munich, translated by M.J. Simpson

At a church service in the Nikolaikirche in Berlin to mark the Day of National Awakening on 21 March, a sermon was preached, summarised in the Nazi press as follows:

4.4

Dr Dibelius based his sermon on the text: If God is for us who can be against us? With these words, he said, the German Parliament was opened on the 4th August 1914. It was a day of the people, one faith began to glow in millions of German hearts and the German people were filled with noble readiness. Today is like that day. A new will for a new German state may be felt everywhere. Today's generation   5 is beginning, like the generation of all wars of liberation, to realise that God is an active God, that God leads us through his grace. And so, taking "With God" as our motto, we will strive towards a new German future.

Völkischer Beobachter, 22 March 1933, Microfilm MZ 9/22, *Institüt für Zeitgeschichte*, Munich, translated by M.J. Simpson

The ease with which the Enabling Act [4.5(a)] was passed may be partially explained by Hitler's appeal for unity. Germany had experienced rule by presidential decree in 1923–24, and again since 1930. The more sinister purpose behind the Enabling Act can perhaps be seen in the comments made at the time by the *Völkischer Beobachter* [4.5(b)].

4.5(a)   The Enabling Act

Reich Law Gazette

1933	Published in Berlin, 24th March 1933

Law concerning the solving of the emergency of the people and the Reich, 24th March 1933.

The Reichstag has issued the following decree, which is hereby announced with the agreement of the Reich Council, after having ensured that the necessary legal constitutional amendments have been made:

Article 1

Laws of the Reich can be passed by the government, in addition to the procedure laid down in the constitution of the Reich. This also applies to laws covered by Articles 85, para 2, and 87 of the Reich constitution.

Article 2

The laws passed by the Reich government do not have to adhere to the constitution provided that the institutions of the Reichstag and Reichsrat have no objection. The rights of the President of the Reich remain unaffected.

Article 3

The laws passed by the government of the Reich will be drafted by the Chancellor and announced in the Law Gazette. They will apply, provided that no other provision is made, from the day following their publication. Articles 68–77 of the constitution do not apply to the laws passed by the government of the Reich.

Article 4

Treaties agreed by the Reich with foreign states, which concern the constitutional affairs of the Reich, do not require the consent of the legislative institutions. The government of the Reich will issue the necessary instructions for the implementation of these treaties.

Article 5

This law applies from the day of its publication. It will expire on the 1st April 1937; it will also be annulled if the present government of the Reich is replaced by another.

Questions on German History, 1984, p. 314

4.5(b)   *Völkischer Beobachter*, 25 March 1933

The will of the German people fulfilled: Parliament hands over power to Adolf Hitler. Passing of the Enabling Law with the overwhelming majority of 441 votes to 94 SPD votes. Unanimous acceptance in the Reichsrat too. Hitler's historic revenge on the men of November. A memorable day in the German Reichstag. Capitulation of the parliamentary system to the new Germany.

Völkischer Beobachter, 25 March, 1933, Microfilm MZ 9/22, *Institut für Zeitgeschichte*, Munich, translated by M.J. Simpsòn

Questions

1 Compare Article 48 in the Weimar Constitution [1.6] with 4.2. Was Hitler observing the letter of the Constitution or its spirit in acting as he did on 28 February 1932?
2 Do you know of any evidence to support Hitler's views on the seriousness of the Communist threat [4.2, 4.3]? Why might he have exaggerated it?
3 Was there anything to suggest that Hitler's undertakings in 4.3 would not be fulfilled?
4 Why should Dr Dibelius have recalled 4 August 1914 in his sermon, and what was the significance of the parallel which he drew [4.4]?
5 In what ways did the Enabling Act increase Hitler's personal powers, as compared with those enjoyed by Brüning [4.5(a, b)]?
6 To what extent were the opposition parties cowed or duped into voting for the Enabling Act?

The elimination of the *Reichstag*'s powers was followed, as we have seen, by the promulgation of 'Laws for the Coordination of the States of the Reich' on 31 March and 7 April. Their effect was to remove the powers of locally elected state governments and to subject the whole of Germany to rule by Nazi *Gauleiters* such as Julius Streicher. The ending of constitutional opposition to the regime was signalled by the law approved by the cabinet on 14 July:

4.6

Art. I The National Socialist German Workers' Party constitutes the only political party in Germany.
Art. II Whoever undertakes to maintain the organisation of another political party shall be punished with penal servitude of up to three years or with imprisonment of between six months and three years, unless the act is subject to a heavier penalty   5
under other regulations.

Nazism, 1919–1945, ed. J. Noakes and G. Pridham, vol. I, 1983, p. 167

As Hindenburg's death approached, Hitler safeguarded his own position, securing cabinet approval for the following decree:

4·7

The Reich Government has enacted the following law which is hereby promulgated.

  Section 1 The office of Reich President will be combined with that of Reich Chancellor. The existing authority of the Reich President will consequently be transferred to the Führer and Reich Chancellor, Adolf Hitler. He will select his deputy.

  Section 2 This law is effective as of the time of the death of Reich President von   5
Hindenburg.

Nazism, 1919–1945, ed. J. Noakes and G. Pridham, vol I, 1983, p. 185

In the campaign preceding the plebiscite which was held on 19 August to approve the merging of the two offices, the *Völkischer Beobachter* made the following appeals to its readers:

4.8(a)

Are you carrying out your highest
duties towards your People?
If so, you are our brother
If not, you are our deadly foe

4.8(b)   An encouragement to vote 'yes' in the plebiscite

The text reads:
'Germans! Think of your children!
Say yes'.

Völkischer Beobachter, **18 August 1934, Bayerischen Staatsbibliothek, Munich**

The results were an impressive victory for Hitler. 95.7% of the 45 million eligible voters went to the polls. More than 38 million voted 'yes', 89.3% of the votes cast. Four-and-a-half million voted 'no'. There were 870,000 spoiled ballot papers.

Behind the velvet glove there was always the threat of the iron fist. There can be no doubt about the violent activities of the *SA* in the election campaign of March 1933. After the decree of 28 February 1933 [4.2] no one was safe from arrest:

4.9 *Völkischer Beobachter*, 21 March 1933

On Wednesday, the first concentration camp will be opened to accommodate 5,000 prisoners. Here, all Communist, and where necessary 'Reichsbanner' and Social Democrat functionaries who endanger state security, will be interned together as their continued stay in state prisons has proved too great a burden. Experience has shown that these people cannot be granted their freedom as they continue to agitate   5 and create unrest when released. In order to ensure state security, we must adopt these measures regardless of any petty considerations. The Police and Ministry of the Interior are convinced that they are thus acting in the national interest and that these measures will have a calculated effect upon the whole nation.

Völkischer Beobachter, 21 March 1933, Microfilm MZ 9/22, *Institut für Zeitgeschichte*, Munich, translated by M.J. Simpson

Questions

1 Should those who voted for Hitler in 1933 have realised that they were voting for a one-party state?
2 Analyse and comment on the arguments used to persuade voters to vote 'yes' in the plebiscite held on 19 August [4.8(a, b)].
3 Account for the huge majority gained by Hitler on this occasion.
4 For what reasons, according to the *Völkischer Beobachter*, were Communists, members of the *Reichsbanner* and Social Democrats arrested?
5 How far was Hitler's dictatorship accepted because of its veneer of legality?

The nature of the Nazi regime

A paradox lies at the heart of Hitler's rule. In theory subject to no constitutional limitations, supported until at least 1938 by huge majorities in the plebiscites he conducted, Hitler's authority would seem to have been absolute. Yet one historian has described Hitler as 'unwilling to take decisions, frequently uncertain, exclusively concerned with upholding his prestige and personal authority, influenced in the strongest fashion by his current entourage, in some respects a weak dictator' (Hans Mommsen, 1971, cited in Ian Kershaw, *The Nazi Dictatorship*, 1985, p. 62). Although the Third Reich appeared to be under the iron control of an absolute dictator and a monolithic party, it has been described as suffering from 'leadership chaos', and Hitler has been accused of producing 'the biggest confusion in government that has ever existed in a civilised state' (Otto Dietrich, Hitler's Press Chief, cited in J. Noakes and G. Pridham (eds.), *Nazism*, vol. II, 1984 p. 205). A new term, 'polycratic', was coined to describe the Nazi system of government. This has been defined as 'a multidimensional power-structure in which Hitler's own authority was only one element (if a very important one)' (Ian Kershaw, *The Nazi Dictatorship*, pp. 65–6).

There can be little dispute over the adulation Hitler received, nor over the limitless powers he enjoyed when he chose to use them [4.10, 4.11]. What remains a matter of dispute is the extent to which Hitler was the originator of policy, and whether he was working towards the goals he had outlined in *Mein Kampf*. One view, held by historians such as Andreas Hillgruber, Karl Dietrich Bracher and Eberhard Jäckel, is indeed that Hitler was the prime mover, both in domestic and foreign policy. 'In Jäckel's opinion, the Nazi regime can be dubbed an '*Alleinherrschaft*' – literally 'sole rule' – which he takes as meaning "that the essential political decisions were taken by a single individual, in this case by Hitler"' (Ian Kershaw, *The Nazi Dictatorship*, p. 65). According to Bracher, so important was the leader principle in Nazi Germany that it is legitimate to equate Nazism with Hitlerism (see K.D. Bracher, *The German Dictatorship*, pp. 423–35). Other historians, notably Martin Broszat and Hans Mommsen, have argued that government under the Nazis disintegrated into a set of competing power bases, notably the Four Year Plan organisation under Göring's control and Himmler's SS empire. Hitler was more of an umpire than a leader, sanctioning policy rather than initiating it. The fragmentation of the decision-making process made for 'improvised bureaucratic initiatives with their own in-built momentum, producing a dynamic process of cumulative radicalization'. This process, Mommsen has argued, partially at least explains the holocaust, where competing groups seized on the Führer's fanatical propaganda utterances as orders for action to prove their diligence and indispensability (Ian Kershaw, *The Nazi Dictatorship*, p. 97).

There is no simple way of reconciling these different viewpoints. The administrative structure of the Third Reich was incredibly complex and untidy. Hitler's predilection was to rule through his trusted henchmen, Göring, Goebbels, Frick, Himmler and Bormann. But he could not dispense with existing elites in the civil service, the army, industry and finance. Thus a dual structure emerged. Existing government departments, for example the Foreign Office, Economic Affairs, Interior, Labour and Agriculture, continued to operate. Superimposed upon them were new Nazi-controlled institutions such as the German Labour Front, the Reich Food Establishment, the six departments set up by Göring to run the Four Year Plan, and the *SS*. There was continual friction over the boundaries of responsibility and no forum where these disagreements could be resolved. The cabinet was never the final source of authority and in any case ceased to meet after 1937. The decision-making process was rarely documented and Hitler's part in it has frequently to be inferred. 4.10–4.14 illustrate the nature and extent of Hitler's authority and describe his style of government. The remaining sections of the chapter are devoted to two areas of policy-making: the handling of the economy and the treatment of the Jews.

4.10 Hitler receiving the congratulations of the *Reichstag* after the *Anschluss* with Austria in March 1938

Imperial War Museum, NYP 68065

While in theory the Weimar Constitution was never abandoned, Hitler's position as *Führer* was made explicit on a number of occasions. In 1938 Hans Frank, head of the Nazi Association of Lawyers and of the Academy of German law, gave a speech in which he said:

4.11

1 At the head of the Reich stands the leader of the *NSDAP* as leader of the German Reich for life.
2 He is, on the strength of being leader of the *NSDAP*, leader and Chancellor of the Reich. As such he embodies simultaneously, as Head of State, supreme State power and, as chief of the government, the central functions of the whole Reich   5
administration. He is Head of State and chief of the Government in one person. He is Commander in Chief of all the armed forces of the Reich.
3 The Führer and Reich Chancellor is the constituent delegate of the German people, who without regard for formal pre-conditions decides the outward form of the Reich, its structure and general policy.   10
4 The Führer is supreme judge of the nation . . . There is no position in the area of constitutional law in the Third Reich independent of the elemental will of the Führer.

Nazism, 1919–1945, ed. J. Noakes and G. Pridham, vol. II, 1984, pp. 199–200

[Hans Frank became the notorious Governor of German-occupied Poland, and was executed as a Nazi war criminal in 1946.]

Questions

1 Charisma has been defined as 'the capacity to inspire followers with devotion and enthusiasm'. How far does **4.10** provide convincing proof of Hitler's charisma?
2 From your own knowledge, compare the powers Hitler enjoyed, according to Frank, with any of the following: (a) a British Prime Minister; (b) an American President; (c) Mussolini; (d) Stalin.
3 In what sense, if at all, was Hitler responsible to the German people?
4 'The Third Reich claimed to be a social, classless community of all Germans and at the same time a superior command structure girded for battle. The function of the leader principle lay in the blending of these two order concepts. It combined the political–charismatic combat idea of the "movement" with the bureaucratic–military order idea of the authoritarian state' (K.D. Bracher). Explain and comment.

4.12, 4.13 and 4.14 give a different slant on the character of Hitler's rule. Fritz Wiedemann, one of Hitler's adjutants, commented as follows on his style of work:

4.12

In 1935 Hitler kept to a reasonably ordered routine . . . Gradually, this fairly orderly work routine broke down. Later Hitler normally appeared shortly before lunch, read quickly through Reich Press Chief Dietrich's press cuttings, and then went into lunch. So it became more and more difficult for Lammers [head of the Reich Chancellery] and Meissner [State Secretary] to get him to make decisions   5
which he alone could make as Head of State . . . When Hitler stayed at the Obersalzburg it was even worse. There, he never left his room before 2.00 p.m. Then he went to lunch. He spent most of his afternoons taking a walk, in the evening straight before dinner, there were films. There can be no question of Hitler's work habits being similar to those attributed to Frederick the Great or   10
Napoleon. He disliked the study of documents. I have sometimes secured decisions from him, even on important matters, without his ever asking to see the relevant files . . .

Nazism, 1919–1945, ed. J. Noakes and G. Pridham, vol. II, 1984, pp. 207–8

Ernst von Weizsäcker, a diplomat of the old school who became State Secretary in the Foreign Office under Neurath and Ribbentrop, had this to say:

4.13

Ministerial skill in the Third Reich consisted in making the most of a favourable hour or minute when Hitler made a decision, this often taking the form of a remark thrown out casually, which then went its way as an 'Order of the Führer'.

A. Bullock, *Hitler, A Study in Tyranny*, 1962, p. 730

A third witness, Albert Speer, was first employed as Hitler's architect before being placed in charge of armaments in 1941. He too had a house at Berchtesgaden, and Hitler's enthusiasm for architecture gave Speer the opportunity to see a great deal of Hitler. Here Speer gives Hitler's own account of his working habits:

4.14

In the first few weeks every petty matter was brought to me for decision. Every day I found heaps of files on my desk, and however much I worked there were always as many again. Finally, I put an end to that nonsense. If I had gone on that way, I would never have accomplished anything, simply because that stuff left me no time for thinking. When I refused to see the files they told me important decisions would   5
be held up. But I decided to clear the decks so I could give my mind to important things. That way I governed the course of development instead of being governed by the officials.

A. Speer, *Inside the Third Reich*, 1970, p. 35

Questions

1 What do Hitler's working habits, as described in **4.12–4.14**, imply about his capacity to make sensible and well-thought-out decisions?
2 Do these accounts support the 'polycratic' or the '*Alleinherrschaft*' view of Hitler's rule?

Economic policy

Economic policy in the Third Reich was the product of a variety of influences. They included Hitler's long-term objectives, the advice of acknowledged experts such as Hjalmar Schacht, and the constraints imposed by external conditions.

The Nazi programme of 1920 listed a number of specific economic policies (see **2.7**), but these appear to have had little influence on Hitler in 1933. He was no economist, and for him economic objectives such as an improvement in living standards were always subordinate to his political goals. He was pledged to defeat unemployment and to improve the condition of the small farmer [**4.1**] in order to win and retain political support. He wanted so far as possible to make Germany economically self-sufficient (autarky) so that she was invulnerable to blockade. He needed a powerful armaments industry. All the evidence suggests that Hitler was willing to employ any means to achieve these ends and that he was neither bound by any preconceived economic theories nor the servant of big business, as some Marxist historians have maintained.

From 1934 until 1937 economic policy was largely in the hands of Schacht, appointed as head of the *Reichsbank* in 1933, and made Economics Minister in 1934 [**4.15**]. A Law to Reduce Unemployment was introduced in June 1933 and the problems of the farmer were addressed in a variety of measures put forward by Walter Darré, who replaced Hugenberg as Minister for Agriculture in June

1933. Schacht's New Plan in 1934 imposed strict controls on imports and sought outlets for German exports through a series of bilateral trade treaties with countries in South America and south-east Europe.

For Hitler the pace of rearmament and the progress of autarky was still too slow. In September 1936 he introduced his own Four Year Plan, and appointed Göring to implement it [4.16]. In 1937 Schacht insisted on resigning as Economics Minister in protest at Göring's policies. He was dismissed from the *Reichsbank* in January 1939, and arrested in 1944 after the July plot against Hitler's life.

The success or failure of Hitler's economic policies has been the subject of much debate. Unemployment was certainly cured, though whether this was due to a natural upturn in the world economy, work-creation schemes or rearmament is open to question. Heavy industry, iron and steel, and chemicals in particular, showed massive growth. The German Labour Front, through its promotion of organisations like 'Strength through Joy' and 'The Beauty of Labour', may have improved working conditions. But real wages barely rose between 1933 and 1939, despite the shortage of labour. Rearmament did not provide the resources for a large-scale war. It has been calculated that in 1939 the army had only six weeks' supply of ammunition as against the six months' recommended by the High Command. A British historian, Tim Mason, has argued that the strains imposed on the German economy by the attempt to provide both guns and butter had produced an economic crisis in 1939 which in its turn helped to persuade Hitler to embark on war as a way out of the impasse (Ian Kershaw, *The Nazi Dictatorship*, pp. 78–81). The statistical evidence is controversial, but the tables in 4.17(a–c) are reliable, so far as they go.

4.15   Schacht's influence on economic policy

As long as I remained in office, whether at the *Reichsbank* or the Ministry of Economics, Hitler never interfered with my work. He never attempted to give me any instructions, but let me carry out my own ideas in my own way and without criticism . . . However, when he realised that the moderation of my financial policy was a stumbling block in his reckless plans (in foreign policy), he began, with Göring's connivance, to go behind my back and counter my arrangements.   5

H. Schacht, *Account Settled*, 1948, pp. 55–6

In August 1936 Hitler composed the following memorandum, which was the basis of the Four Year Plan. The document came to light only through Albert Speer, who received one of the three copies:

4.16   Memorandum on the Four Year Plan, August 1936

The Political Situation

Since the outbreak of the French Revolution the world has been moving with ever-increasing-speed towards a new conflict, the most extreme solution of which is Bolshevism; and the essence and goal of Bolshevism is the elimination of those social strata which have hitherto provided the leadership and their replacement by world wide Jewry . . .   5

Germany

Germany will as always have to be regarded as the focus of the Western world against the attacks of Bolshevism. I do not regard this as an agreeable mission but as a serious handicap and burden for our national life. We cannot, however, escape this   10
destiny . . . Nearly four precious years have now gone by. There is no doubt that by now we could have been completely independent of foreign countries in the spheres of fuel supplies, rubber supplies, and partly also iron ore supplies. Just as we are now producing 700,000 or 800,000 tons of petroleum, we could be producing 3 million tons. Just as we are manufacturing a few thousand tons of rubber, we   15
could already be producing 70,000 or 80,000 tons per annum. Just as we have stepped up the production of iron ore from $2\frac{1}{2}$ million tons to 7 million tons, we could process 20 or 25 million tons of German iron ore and even 30 million tons if necessary. There has been time enough in four years to find out what we cannot do. Now we have to carry out what we can do.   20

I thus set the following tasks:
I The German armed forces must be operational within four years.
II The German economy must be fit for war within four years.

Nazism, 1919–1945, ed. J. Noakes and G. Pridham, vol. II, 1984, pp. 280–87

The following tables have been selected to illustrate (a) Germany's economic recovery under the Nazis; (b) the role played by public spending in helping to cure unemployment; and (c) the impact of the Four Year Plan.

4.17(a)   Statistics of recovery in Germany, 1928–38

	1928	1932	1933	1934	1935	1936	1937	1938
GNP (1928 prices) RM bn	89.5	71.9	73.7	83.7	92.3	101.2	114.2	126.2
Industrial production (1928 = 100)	100	58	66	83	96	107	117	122
Unemployment (million)		1.4	5.6	4.8	2.7	2.2	1.6	0.9	0.4

RM = Reichsmark

R.J. Overy, *The Nazi Economic Recovery, 1932–1938*, 1982, p. 29

4.17(b)   Public expenditure in Germany by category, 1928–38 (bn RM)*

	1928	1932	1933	1934	1935	1936	1937	1938
Total expenditure (central and local)	23.2	17.1	18.4	21.6	21.9	23.6	26.9	37.1
Construction	2.7	0.9	1.7	3.5	4.9	5.4	6.1	7.9
Rearmament	0.7	0.7	1.8	3.0	5.4	10.2	10.9	17.2
Transportation	2.6	0.8	1.3	1.8	2.1	2.4	2.7	3.8
Work creation	—	0.2	1.5	2.5	0.8	—	—	—

Note: *There is some overlap between the categories. Work creation included some expenditure on roads; construction also included some rearmament expenditure.

R.J. Overy, *The Nazi Economic Recovery, 1932–1938*, 1982, p.50

4.17(c)   Output of selected commodities under the Four Year Plan

(in thousands of tons)

	1936 output	1938 output	1942 output	Plan target
Mineral oil*	1,790	2,340	6,260	13,830
Aluminium	98	166	260	273
Buna rubber	0.7	5	96	120
Nitrogen	770	914	930	1,040
Explosives	18	45	300	223
Steel	19,216	22,656	20,480	24,000
Iron ore	2,255	3,360	4,137	5,549
Brown coal	161,382	194,985	245,918	240,500
Hard coal	158,400	186,186	166,059	213,000

Note: *Including synthetic production of petroleum.

In general, by the outbreak of war Germany was still dependent on foreign sources of supply for one third of her raw material requirements.

Nazism, 1919–1945, ed. J. Noakes and G. Pridham, vol. II, 1984, pp. 290–92

Questions

1 What light do **4.15** and **4.16** shed on the argument that Hitler was in some senses 'a weak dictator'?
2 Compare Hitler's guesstimates in **4.16** with the output of selected commodities actually achieved under the Four Year Plan. What do they suggest about Hitler's view of Germany's industrial potential?
3 Does the evidence provided by **4.16** and **4.17(a–c)** prove that after 1936 preparation for war took precedence over all other economic objectives? Explain your answer.

Nazi policy towards the Jews

All serious historians of the Nazi period are united in their abhorrence of the anti-Jewish policies of the Third Reich. The holocaust can have no apologists. An essential prelude to the holocaust, however, was the climate of anti-Semitism which the Nazi regime encouraged, but also reflected. This reciprocal relationship between Nazism and the latent anti-Semitism in some quarters of German society raises problems about responsibility for the anti-Jewish policies which culminated in the Final Solution. While there can be no dispute about Hitler's detestation of the Jewish race and his willingness to encourage hostility to the Jews (see **2.10(e, f)**), it is not always clear who took the initiative in the anti-Semitic policies adopted between 1933 and 1939. Indeed, there were even times, it seems, when for tactical reasons Hitler tried to restrain the tiger of anti-Semitism which he had deliberately unleashed. The same problem arises over responsibility for the Final Solution, which will be addressed in chapter 6. **4.18** and **4.20** illustrate the climate of hostility which enveloped the Jewish race in Nazi Germany. **4.19** and **4.21–4.23** document the specific policies adopted by the Nazi regime towards the Jews.

Der Stürmer was founded as an anti-Jewish newspaper in 1923 by Julius Streicher, a schoolteacher from Nuremberg who joined the Nazi party in that year. Streicher was a favourite of Hitler's; he was appointed *Gauleiter* of Franconia-Nuremburg and acted as official host at party Congresses. Every issue of *Der Stürmer* (a weekly magazine) contained anti-Jewish cartoons. **4.18** is a typical example.

4.18 *Der Stürmer*, March 1932

Jn Deutschland

Vater, warum müffen wir zuhaufe fo frieren, wo es doch foviele Kohlen gibt?
Weil die Hand Juda fchwer auf dem Volke liegt!

The text reads: 'Father, why must we freeze at home when there is so much coal? Because the hand of the Jew lies heavily on the people!'

Der Stürmer, March 1932, Bayerischen Staatsbibliothek, Munich

Between 1933 and 1939 Jews were subjected to increasing violence and discrimination, though the process was haphazard and unco-ordinated. It began with a boycott of Jewish shops and professions [4.19] and the removal of Jews from the civil service [4.21], both in April 1933.

4.19 Call from the leadership of the *NSDAP*

Boycott Committees against the Jews throughout the whole Reich. On 1 April, at the stroke of ten, the boycott of all Jewish businesses, doctors, lawyers begins – ten thousand mass gatherings. The Jews have declared war on 65 millions, now they are to be hit where it hurts them most.

Völkischer Beobachter, 30 March 1933, Microfilm MZ 9/22, *Institut für Zeitgeschichte*, Munich, translated by M.J. Simpson

4.20   Anti-Jewish banner in Rosenheim

Rosenheim is a small village in Bavaria about thirty miles from Munich. The words on the
bunting read: 'Jews are not welcome here!'

Imperial War Museum, MH 133348

**4.21   Law for the Restoration of the Professional Civil Service,
7 April 1933**

III.1 Officials who are of non-Aryan descent [this came to mean persons with only
one non-Aryan grandparent and those married to non-Aryans] are to be retired;
honorary officials are to be dismissed from office.

2 Section 1 does not apply to officials who were already in service on 1 August,
1914, or who fought in the world war at the front for the German Reich, or whose   5
fathers or sons were killed in the first world war.

Nazism, 1919–1945, ed. J. Noakes and G. Pridham, vol. II, 1984, pp. 223–4

There were no further official moves against Jews until September 1935. There was a wave of anti-Semitic boycotts and violence in the summer of 1935, locally inspired but privately encouraged by Goebbels and Streicher. The Ministry of the Interior had also been considering the definition of Jewishness and bans on mixed marriages. At the Nuremberg Rally in September 1935 Hitler, having cancelled an important foreign-policy speech, evidently decided to appease the party faithful by a further batch of anti-Jewish measures. The Ministry of the Interior was instructed to produce at two days' notice laws forbidding marriage and sexual relations between Jews and Aryans, and a definition of citizenship which would exclude Jews.

The Nuremberg Laws were duly promulgated on 15 September 1935.

4.22(a)   Law for the Protection of German Blood and Honour

Entirely convinced that the purity of German blood is essential to the further existence of the German people, and inspired by the uncompromising determination to safeguard the future of the German nation, the *Reichstag* has unanimously adopted the following law, which is promulgated herewith:
1 Marriages between Jews and citizens of German or kindred blood are forbidden . . .   5
2 Sexual relations outside marriage between Jews and nationals of German or kindred blood are forbidden.

Nazism, 1919–1945, ed. J. Noakes and G. Pridham, vol. II, 1984, p. 535

4.22(b)   Reich Citizenship Law of 15 September 1935

I.1 A subject of the State is a person who belongs to the protective union of the German Reich, and who therefore has particular obligations towards the Reich.
   2 The status of subject is acquired in accordance with the provisions of the Reich and State Law of citizenship.
II.1 A citizen of the Reich is that subject only who is of German or kindred blood   5
and who, through his conduct, shows that he is both desirous and fit to serve the German people and Reich faithfully.

Nazism, 1919–1945, ed. J. Noakes and G. Pridham, vol. II, 1984, pp. 535–6

There was much debate over the classification of a Jew, Hitler evidently favouring as inclusive a definition as possible (i.e. the possession of one Jewish grandparent). On this occasion the moderates prevailed, and under a law approved on 14 November 1935 those of mixed blood, i.e. with one or two non-Jewish grandparents, were entitled to German citizenship, albeit of a restricted kind.

There was another pause in official policy in 1936–37, mainly it would seem to reassure foreign opinion and to improve Germany's image during the Berlin Olympic Games in 1936. But Hitler again vented his spleen against the Jews at the Nuremberg Rally of September 1937. In April 1938 Göring insisted on the registration of all Jewish property, and in July all Jews were required to identify themselves by having recognised Jewish first names.

4.23   Decree, 17 July 1938

I.1 Jews must be given only such first names as are specified in the directives issued by the Reich Minister of the Interior concerning the bearing of the first name.

2 Section I does not apply to Jews of foreign nationality.

II.1 If Jews bear first names other than those authorised for Jews by Section I, they   5
must from 1 January 1939, adopt another additional first name, namely 'Israel' for men and 'Sarah' for women.

Nazism, 1919–1945, ed. J. Noakes and G. Pridham, vol. II, 1984, p. 553

Questions

1 Compare 4.18 and 4.20 as evidence for the incidence of popular anti-Semitism in Germany. Which would you regard as the more damaging?
2 To what extent do the anti-Jewish policies adopted between 1933 and 1938 reflect the ideas contained in *Mein Kampf* [2.10(e, f), 4.19 and 4.21–4.23]?
3 What evidence can you find from 4.19 and 4.21–4.23 that the Nazi leadership was divided in its views about the treatment of the Jews?
4 How do you account for the growing harshness of the policies adopted?

The most violent expression of anti-Jewish sentiment prior to the war arose out of a chance incident. On 7 November 1938 Herschel Grynspan shot dead Ernst von Rath, a secretary in the German embassy in Paris. Grynspan, a Polish Jew, was anxious to avenge the forcible deportation of his parents to Poland. At a reunion of those concerned in the Munich *putsch* Goebbels seized on this event as an excuse to suggest a co-ordinated campaign of terror against the Jews. Hitler gave his approval. On *Kristallnacht*, 9/10 November 1938, so christened because of the thousands of Jewish shop-windows that were smashed, even according to Nazi figures 815 shops were destroyed, 191 synagogues set on fire and 76 synagogues demolished; 91 Jews were killed, 20,000 arrested. While official involvement was never admitted, enough evidence has since come to light to suggest that the events of *Kristallnacht* were orchestrated by the Nazi party [4.24(a, b)]. To add insult to injury, Göring required Jews to meet the cost of damage to their property themselves, and on 12 November 1938 the

Jewish community was ordered to pay a fine of 1 billion *Reichsmarks* to assist in the furtherance of the Four Year Plan.

On the same day a decree was issued barring Jews from owning or managing businesses.

4.24(a)   A secret report prepared by the Nazi party Supreme Court after the events of 9–10 November 1938

On the evening of 9 November 1938, Reich Propaganda Director and Party Member Dr Goebbels told the Party leaders assembled at a social evening in the old town hall in Munich that in the districts of Kurhessen and Magdeburg-Anhalt there had been anti-Jewish demonstrations during which Jewish shops were demolished and synagogues were set on fire. The Führer at Goebbels' suggestion had decided   5
that such demonstrations were not to be prepared or organised by the Party, but neither were they to be discouraged if they originated spontaneously . . .

The oral instructions of the Reich Propaganda Director were probably understood by all the Party leaders present to mean that the Party should not outwardly appear as the originator of the demonstrations but that in reality it should organise   10
them and carry them out. Instructions in this sense were telephoned immediately (and therefore a considerable time before the transmission of the first teletype) to the bureaux of their districts by a large number of the Party members present . . .

Nazism, 1919–1945, ed. J. Noakes and G. Pridham, vol. II, 1984, pp. 553–5

Among the instructions sent out was this from the *Reichssicherheitshauptamt* (*RSHA* – The Reich Central Bureau for Security):

4.24(b)

Only such measures may be employed as will not endanger German lives or property – for example, synagogues may only be burnt when there is no risk that fire will spread to neighbouring structures. Jewish stores and dwellings may be destroyed but not plundered . . . The police must not interfere with the demonstrations that will occur . . . only as many Jews – particularly wealthy ones –   5
should be arrested as can be accommodated in available jails. After completion of the arrests contact should promptly be established with the appropriate concentration camp to provide for immediate transfer of Jews . . .

B. Engelmann, *In Hitler's Germany*, 1988, p. 113

Questions

1 What was Hitler's role in prompting the events of *Kristallnacht*?
2 How far do you think popular anti-Semitism contributed to the destruction of Jewish lives and property on *Kristallnacht*?

5 The foreign policy of the Third Reich

Hitler's aims

The foreign policy of the Third Reich between 1933 and 1945 is the subject of as much controversy as its domestic policies. Many of the same arguments recur. Was Hitler pursuing the goals he had set out in *Mein Kampf*, as many historians would still assert? (See for instance Andreas Hillgruber, *Hitlers Strategie, Politik und Kriegsführung*, 1965); or was he an opportunist, 'a man of improvisation and experiment, and the spur of the moment bright idea' (Hans Mommsen, cited in Ian Kershaw, *The Nazi Dictatorship*, 1985, p. 171)?

The debates over the polycratic nature of Hitler's rule extend also to his foreign policy. Though it is generally accepted that Hitler was much more interested in foreign affairs than he was in domestic policy, some would argue that he was still an arbitrator between competing pressure groups, the army, the Foreign Office and the Nazi party for instance, and that at certain times he was under the influence of key advisers such as Göring and Ribbentrop.

Hitler's foreign policy includes another set of variables, the policies of the leaders of other countries with whom Hitler had to deal. This introduces another dimension to the argument about responsibility. A.J.P. Taylor has gone so far as to say that the outbreak of the Second World War may have owed as much to the 'faults and failures of European statesmen' as it did to Hitler's ambitions (A.J.P. Taylor, *The Origins of the Second World War*, 1964, pp. 265–6).

There is, finally, a lively debate over the continuity of German foreign policy. Fritz Fischer resurrected this debate with his work on the origins of the First World War, *Griff nach der Weltmacht* (Grasping for World Power), published in 1961. Fischer maintains that the objective of a Greater Germany – the domination of Eastern Europe – 'originated during the *Kaiserreich* [The German empire, 1871–1918], led to the First World War, seemed to find realisation in the peace of Brest Litovsk, lay dormant during the interregnum of the Weimar Republic (which continued to call itself the German empire) and gathered momentum during the Third Reich and into the Second World War' (F. Fischer, *From Kaiserreich to Third Reich. Elements of Continuity in German History, 1871–1945*, 1986, p. 97).

This chapter cannot hope to explain all these rival viewpoints and perspectives, but they should be borne in mind when you look at the documentary evidence.

We begin with an analysis of Hitler's long-term goals. The evidence is drawn from *Mein Kampf*, volumes I and II, and from *Hitler's Secret Book*. The latter was written between May and July 1928, discovered in 1945 and first published in 1958. The incoherent structure of *Mein Kampf* means that references to foreign policy are scattered throughout the book. The *Secret Book* is primarily concerned with foreign policy and could be said to give a more considered view of what Hitler took to be Germany's proper international role. For the sake of clarity, references to both books have been grouped under common headings. Curiously, there are no direct references to the Treaty of Versailles, but 5.1(a) indicates well enough Hitler's opinion of it.

5.1(a)   The Treaty of Versailles

What could have been done with this Treaty of Versailles?! This instrument of boundless extortion and abject humiliation might, in the hands of a willing government, have become an instrument for whipping up the nationalist passions to fever heat. With a brilliant propagandist exploitation of these sadistic cruelties, the indifference of a people might have been raised to indignation, and indignation to   5
blazing fury!

How could every single one of these points have been burned into the brain and emotion of this people, until finally in sixty million heads, in men and women, a common sense of shame and a common hatred would have become a single fiery sea of flame from whose heat a will as hard as steel would have risen and a cry burst   10
forth:
  Give us arms! . . .
All this was neglected and nothing was done . . .

Adolf Hitler, *Mein Kampf*, translated by Ralph Manheim, 1969, p. 577

5.1(b)   *Lebensraum*

(i)   Germany has an annual increase in population of nearly nine hundred thousand souls. The difficulty of feeding this army of new citizens must grow greater from year to year and ultimately end in catastrophe, unless ways and means are found to forestall the danger of starvation and misery in time. [Hitler goes on to look at four possible solutions: birth control, internal colonisation, territorial   5
expansion and industrial and commercial development.]

The acquisition of new soil for the settlement of the excess population possesses an infinite number of advantages, particularly if we turn from the present to the future . . . it must be said that such a territorial policy cannot be fulfilled in the

Cameroons, but almost exclusively in Europe . . . If this earth really has room for all   10
to live in, let us be given the soil we need for our livelihood.

True, they will not willingly do this. But the law of self-preservation goes into
effect; and what is refused to amicable methods, it is up to the fist to take. If our
forefathers had let their decisions depend on the same pacific nonsense as our
contemporaries, we should possess only a third of our present territory;   15
(ii)   And so we National Socialists consciously draw a line beneath the foreign
policy tendency of the pre-War period. We take up where we broke off six hundred
years ago. We stop the endless German movement to the south and west, and turn
our gaze to the land in the east. At long last we break off the colonial and
commercial policy of the pre-war period and shift to the soil policy of the future.

**Adolf Hitler, *Mein Kampf*, translated by Ralph Manheim, 1969,
pp. 120–27, 598**

5.1(c)   The attack on Jews and Bolsheviks

See **2.10(f)** and **4.16**.

5.1(d)   Alliance policy

(i)   England desires no Germany as a world power, but France wishes no power at
all called Germany: quite an essential difference, after all! Today we are not fighting
for a position as a world power; today we must struggle for the existence of our
fatherland, for the unity of our nation and the daily bread of our children. If we
look about us for European allies, from this standpoint, there remain only two   5
states: England and Italy.

Adolf Hitler, *Mein Kampf*, translated by Ralph Manheim, 1969, p. 565

(ii)   Since the year 1920 I have tried with all means and most persistently to
accustom the National Socialist movement to the idea of an alliance among
Germany, Italy and England.

Hitler's Secret Book, ed. Telford Taylor, 1961, p. 166

Questions

1 How do Hitler's views on the Treaty of Versailles differ, if at all, from those
   of his German contemporaries [**1.18–1.20**]?
2 According to Hitler, what mistakes have the Weimar governments committed in relation to the Treaty of Versailles?
3 What are the implications of Hitler's views on *Lebensraum* [**5.1(b)**] for his
   conduct of international relations? Should western statesmen have been
   more prepared to take his words at their face value?

4 Explain the reference to 'the colonial and commercial policy of the pre-war period' [5.1(b)(ii), lines 19–20].
5 Is it possible from the sources cited in 5.1(b) to detect precisely where Germany's new living space was to be found?
6 Did Hitler have any rational grounds for linking the Jewish to the Bolshevik threat [2.10(f), 4.16]? Did either threat have any substance?
7 Why did Hitler advocate alliances with England and Italy?

What was the relationship between the objectives referred to in 5.1 and the policies actually pursued? In the *'Second Thoughts'*, which preface A.J.P. Taylor's second edition of *The Origins of the Second World War*, he describes Hitler as 'The abstract speculator' who 'turned out to be also a statesman on the make who did not consider beforehand what he would make or how' (A.J.P. Taylor, *Origins of the Second World War*, 1964, p. 25). H.R. Trevor-Roper, on the other hand, sees a consistency of purpose running through all Hitler's policies and argues that 'the importance of *Mein Kampf* as a real declaration of Hitler's considered and practical war aims, even in 1924, is often overlooked' (cited in H.W. Koch (ed.) *Aspects of the Third Reich*, 1985, p. 238). To test the validity of these contrasting views we need to be clear first about the actual course of German foreign policy and secondly about Hitler's role in the making of it.

In October 1933 Germany left the Disarmament Conference at Geneva and the League of Nations, actions which won overwhelming approval in a subsequent plebiscite. In January 1934 Hitler signed a Non-Aggression Treaty with Poland, and ordered an end to the military and economic co-operation with the Soviet Union which had been in operation since the Treaty of Rapallo, 1921. In January 1935 inhabitants of the Saar, an industrial area west of the Rhine which had been placed under the control of the League of Nations, voted, again by an overwhelming majority, to return to the Reich. In March of that year Hitler introduced conscription, in open defiance of the Treaty of Versailles. In June he reached a Naval Agreement with England which allowed Germany to build up to 35 per cent of British tonnage in capital ships and the same number of submarines, again contrary to the Treaty of Versailles [5.2]. In March 1936 German troops occupied the demilitarised zone in the Rhineland, in breach of both the Treaty of Versailles and the Treaty of Locarno. On the outbreak of the Spanish Civil War in July 1936 Hitler agreed to send military aid to General Franco, the fascist usurper of the Spanish Republican government.

In October 1936 Protocols were signed with Italy, a prelude to the Rome–

Berlin Axis, 'this vertical line between Rome and Berlin . . . around which all the European States animated by the will to collaboration and peace can also collaborate', which Mussolini announced in November. In the same month Germany and Japan signed the Anti-Comintern Pact. This committed the signatories to work together to combat Communist subversion. Italy joined the following year. No new initiatives took place in 1937, but Hitler held a critical meeting with his service chiefs on 5 November at which he spelt out his aggressive designs on Austria and Czechoslovakia [5.6].

In March 1938 German troops crossed the Austrian border, and the *Anschluss* with Austria was accomplished. The summer of 1938 was dominated by the Czech crisis, which culminated in the Munich Agreement on 30 September providing for the return of the Sudetenland to Germany [5.7–5.11]. In March 1939 Germany occupied the remainder of Czechoslovakia. Bohemia was absorbed into the Reich while Slovakia became a German protectorate. At the same time, under threat of bombardment the Lithuanian government also agreed to the transfer of the Memel to Germany.

In April preparations for the invasion of Poland were ordered. On 22 May Hitler signed a 'Pact of Steel' with Mussolini. On 23 August Hitler announced the signature of the Nazi–Soviet Pact. On 1 September German troops invaded Poland [5.12–5.18]. In October, following the defeat of Poland, Hitler ordered his generals to prepare an attack on France and the Low Countries. This was duly launched in May 1940. In July, shortly after the capitulation of France in June, Hitler gave instructions to prepare for the invasion of Russia. On 27 September the Anti-Comintern Pact was transformed into a Tripartite Pact with Italy and Japan. The decision to go ahead with Operation Barbarossa, the invasion of Russia, was taken on 18 December. In April 1941 German troops invaded Yugoslavia and Greece, and on 22 June 1941 they crossed the Russian frontier [5.19–5.27]. When the United States declared war on Japan, following the Japanese attack on the American fleet at Pearl Harbour, Hitler had no hesitation in declaring war on the United States, and what had been a European war became a world war. As a result about 52 million people suffered death, including 7 million Germans and the 6 million Jews who were deliberately killed.

It is hard to dispute that Hitler's nebulous ambitions were translated into hard reality. The Treaty of Versailles was demolished; Germans in Austria, Czechoslovakia and Poland were incorporated into the *Reich*; *Lebensraum* was sought and won in Poland and the Ukraine. All-out war was declared both on Jews and Bolsheviks. At the same time there were some obvious departures from the methods, if not the ultimate goals, listed in *Mein Kampf*. The alliance with Italy may have been secured, but the search for an alliance with England, on which Hitler set so much store, was abandoned. There are evident inconsistencies in the policies pursued towards Austria, Czechoslovakia and Poland between 1934 and 1939; most obviously there is the startling contrast between the Anti-Comintern Pact of 1936 and the Nazi–Soviet Pact of 1939. Critics of the 'intentionalist' school have seized on these inconsistencies; they have also argued that war might have been averted had Western statesmen acted differently, notably in the Czech and Polish crises of 1938 and 1939. Finally it has been contended that the war against Russia which broke out in 1941 was as much due to Soviet as it was to German ambitions. It is to these areas of controversy that we now turn.

The alliance with England

There can be little doubt that until 1937 Hitler continued to work for good relations with England. His instructions to the negotiators of the Anglo-German Naval Agreement in 1935 stated:

5.2

An understanding must be reached between the two great Germanic peoples through the permanent elimination of naval rivalry. One will control the sea, the other will be the strongest power on land. A defensive and offensive alliance between the two will inaugurate a new era.

Nazism, 1919–1945, ed. J. Noakes and G. Pridham, vol. III, 1988, p. 667

In December 1936 Ribbentrop, who had negotiated the Naval Agreement, was appointed ambassador to Britain. He was instructed to do his best to get Britain into the Anti-Comintern Pact.

5.3

Ribbentrop . . . get Britain to join the Anti-Comintern Pact, that is what I want most of all. I have sent you as the best man I've got. Do what you can . . . But if in future all our efforts are still in vain, fair enough, then I'm ready for war as well. I would regret it very much, but if it has to be, there it is.

Nazism, 1919–1945, ed. J. Noakes and G. Pridham, vol. III, 1988, p. 673

Ribbentrop had little success, and by the end of 1937 had clearly concluded that Britain would oppose any significant change in the balance of power in Germany's favour.

On 6 November 1937, after Italy had been brought into the Anti-Comintern Pact, Ribbentrop wrote in his diary:

5.4

Three peoples are pledging themselves to go the same way, the way which will possibly lead to war, to a necessary war, if one is to crack this shell which is stifling the energy and the aims of these emergent nations.

W. Michalka, 'From the Anti-Comintern Pact to the Euro-Asiatic Bloc', *Aspects of the Third Reich*, ed. H.W. Koch, 1985, p. 268

Ribbentrop summarised his views on Anglo-German relations in a Note which he prepared for the Führer, dated 2 January 1938:

5.5

5 We must draw the following conclusions:
  1) Outwardly our declared policy should be an understanding with England, while protecting the interests of our friends.
  2) Construction secretly, but with absolute determination, of a network of alliances against England, i.e. in practice a strengthening of friendship with Italy and Japan . . .
6 The particular question of whether, in the event of Germany becoming involved in a conflict in Central Europe, France and thus England will intervene depends on the circumstances and timing of the outbreak of such a conflict and on military considerations which cannot be assessed here. I have some points to make orally to the Führer on this.

Nazism, 1919–1945, ed. J. Noakes and G. Pridham, vol. III, 1988, pp. 695–6

Questions

1 'It may be that we are on a road leading to war. If that is so, then this agreement is tantamount to erecting a danger sign on the road ahead' (Stanley Baldwin). Compare this perception of the Anglo-German Naval Agreement with Hitler's [5.2].
2 How did Ribbentrop's views differ from Hitler's, and what impression do you get of his influence on Hitler [5.3–5.5]?
3 Account for the worsening of Anglo-German relations between 1935 and January 1938.

Responsibility for the outbreak of war, 1937–39

In gauging Hitler's intentions from 1937 to 1939 and assessing Hitler's responsibilty for the outbreak of war in 1939, much attention has been devoted to the so-called Hossbach Memorandum. This document has a curious history. It was written by Friedrich Hossbach, Hitler's Adjutant at the time, and describes a meeting held between Hitler and the three heads of the armed services – Göring (airforce), Fritsch (army) and Raeder (navy). Blomberg (Minister for Defence) and Neurath (Foreign Minister) were also present. The meeting took place on 5 November 1937, but Hossbach, on his own admission, wrote his account five days later, though whether from memory or on the basis of notes made at the time is still not clear. It was sent to Blomberg for filing. Hitler never saw it, claiming, according to A.J.P. Taylor, that he was too busy to read it. The original disappeared, but a copy was made by a certain Colonel von Kirchbach, who gave it to a relative. A second copy, though not an exact one, was forwarded to the prosecution team at Nuremberg in 1945. Hossbach himself published his own version in 1948 in his memoirs, *Zwischen Wehrmacht und Hitler* (Between the Wehrmacht and Hitler). The text runs to six and a half pages, and is the familiar Hitlerian jumble of wild assertion and cloudy speculation. The following passages relate to Hitler's objectives:

5.6   The Hossbach Memorandum, November 1937

Hitler 'wished to explain to the gentlemen present his basic ideas concerning the opportunities for the development of our position in the field of foreign affairs and its requirements, and he asked, in the interests of a long-term German policy, that his exposition be regarded, in the event of his death, as his last will and testament'.

'The aim of German policy was to make secure and to preserve the racial   5
community and to enlarge it. It was therefore a question of space. The question for Germany was: where could it achieve the greatest gain at the lowest cost?'
[Hitler then considered three contingencies:
1 The period 1943–45. After this period the balance of world power would shift to Germany's disadvantage.] 'It was while the rest of the world was fencing itself off   10
that we were obliged to take the offensive. If the Führer was still living, it was his unalterable determination to solve Germany's problem of space by 1943–45 at the latest.'
[Contingencies 2 and 3 postulated respectively internal strife in France and French embroilment in war that would prevent her 'proceeding' against Germany. In either   15
case Germany should take action against the Czechs:]

'For the improvement of our politico-military position our first objective, in the event of our being embroiled in war, must be to overthrow Czechoslovakia and Austria simultaneously in order to remove the threat to our flank in any possible operation against the West.'   20

[Hitler then went on to consider the likely reactions of other countries to a German attack on Czechoslovakia and Austria. He postulated a possible war between Italy and France allied to Britain, and concluded:]

'If Germany made use of this war to settle the Czech and Austrian questions, it was to be assumed that Britain, herself at war with Italy, would decide not to act   20 against Germany. Without British support, no warlike action by France against Germany was to be expected.

'The time for our attack on the Czechs and Austria must be made dependent on the course of the Anglo–French–Italian war . . . This descent upon the Czechs would have to be carried out with "lightning speed".'

Nazism, 1919–1945, ed. J. Noakes and G. Pridham, vol. III, 1988, pp. 680–87

A.J.P. Taylor, criticised for discounting the importance of the Hossbach Memorandum in the first edition of his *Origins of the Second World War*, was unrepentant, and in 1965 declared that the meeting 'had no significance'.

There were no immediate consequences to the Hossbach Memorandum, but on 7 December General Jodl, Chief of Operations Staff at Army High Command changed the army's plans to give them a more aggressive slant. An invasion of Czechoslovakia was now conceived not as a pre-emptive strike against France's ally but as an offensive war.

5.7   War on two fronts with main effort in south-east 'Operation Green'

When Germany has achieved complete preparedness for war in all spheres, then the military conditions will have been created for carrying out an offensive war against Czechoslovakia, so that the solution of the German problem of living space can be carried to a victorious conclusion even if one or another of the Great Powers intervene against us.

Nazism, 1919–1945, ed. J. Noakes and G. Pridham, vol. III, 1988, p. 691

Questions

1 To what extent do you think the Hossbach Memorandum is an accurate record of what transpired on 5 November 1937?
2 Does the fact that Contingencies 2 and 3 never transpired invalidate the Hossbach Memorandum as a guide to Hitler's objectives?
3 What connections can you see between *Mein Kampf* and the Hossbach Memorandum?
4 Do you think there is a direct connection between the Hossbach Memorandum and 5.7?

German achievements in 1938 bore an uncanny resemblance to the objectives of the Hossbach Memorandum, even if none of the scenarios Hitler had painted actually materialised. In February the Austrian premier, Schuschnigg, sought Hitler's assistance in controlling the activities of Austrian Nazis who were threatening a coup. Hitler imposed harsh terms in return for agreeing to support Schuschnigg's government, including the appointment of the Nazi leader Seyss-Inquart to the Ministry of the Interior. On 9 March, however, Schuschnigg repented of his concessions and announced a plebiscite on Austria's independence. Göring urged immediate intervention. Hitler, concerned over Mussolini's reaction to a German invasion (he had strongly opposed German intervention in Austria in 1934), sent a special envoy, Philip of Hesse, to secure Mussolini's acquiescence. In Berlin Göring had largely taken over the handling of the crisis, and it was on his instructions that invasion was threatened. Such was the popular reception given to Hitler and to the German troops who entered Austria on 12 March that the integration of Austria into the Reich was decided on then and there. The exact form of the *Anschluss* may not have been premeditated. It had been an objective ever since the setting up of the Weimar Republic.

Between March and September 1938 all European eyes were fixed on Czechoslovakia. Hitler's immediate objectives are hard to discern, and indeed they may have changed from week to week. He certainly wanted the Sudetenland. Opinions are divided on whether he was bluffing when he threatened to go to war to get it, and on whether he was aiming at acquiring the whole of Czechoslovakia at this stage.

On 28 March Henlein, the Nazi leader of the Sudeten Germans, was instructed to 'demand so much that we can never be satisfied'. But on 20 May Hitler indicated that 'it was not my intention to smash Czechoslovakia by military action in the immediate future without provocation . . .' Rumours of German military activity then led to partial Czech mobilisation and this seems to have been decisive in causing Hitler to change his mind. At a meeting with his military leaders on 28 May he ordered Operation Green to be put into effect in the near future, as Jodl recorded:

5.8

II   War on two fronts with main effort in South-East
(strategic concentration 'Green')

1 Political Assumptions: It is my unalterable decision to smash Czechoslovakia by
military action in the near future. It is the business of the political leadership to
await or bring about the suitable moment from a political and military point of view.   5
[A covering letter from Keitel, now Hitler's Chief of Staff, gave 1 October as the
date by which the plan was to be executed.]

Nazism, 1919–1945, ed. J. Noakes and G. Pridham, vol. III, 1988, p. 712

The premiers of Britain and France, Chamberlain and Daladier, ignorant of
Hitler's orders, urged the Czechs to cede the Sudetenland. Hitler had three
meetings with Chamberlain, at Berchtesgaden on 15 September, at Bad
Godesburg on 22–23 September, and at Munich on 29–30 September. Hitler
first accepted Chamberlain's offer of the Sudetenland (Berchtesgaden), then
insisted on immediate German military occupation (Bad Godesburg), and was
finally persuaded at Munich to accept a phased occupation, accompanied by an
international commission to decide on disputed boundaries. Some light on
Hitler's real intentions is shed by the following comment in Ernst von
Weizsäcker's diary. Weizsäcker, a career diplomat, had been appointed
Secretary of State to Ribbentrop in February 1938. His papers were published
in 1974.

5.9   Weizsäcker's diary, 9 October 1938

We appeared to have won the game when Chamberlain announced his visit to the
Obersalzburg in order to preserve peace. This represented a rejection of crisis
politics. One could have reached an agreement without difficulty, on the basis of
English mediation, about how the Sudetenland was to be split off and transferred to
us in a peaceful manner.   5
  However we were dominated by the determination to have a war of revenge and
destruction against Czechoslovakia. Thus, we conducted a second phase of
discussions with Chamberlain at Bad Godesburg in such a way that, despite our
agreement, what had been decided was bound to fail. The group who wanted war,
namely Ribbentrop and the *SS*, had nearly succeeded in prompting the Führer to   10
attack. Among the numerous similar statements made by the Führer in my presence
during the night of 27–28 September was one to the effect that he would now
annihilate Czechoslovakia. Ribbentrop and I were the sole witnesses of these words;
they were not designed to have an effect on a third party.
  Thus the assumption that the Führer was intending a huge bluff is incorrect. His   15
resentment stemming from May 22, when the English accused him of pulling back,

led him on to the path of war. I have not quite managed to establish what influences then finally decided him to issue invitations to the four-power meeting in Munich on 28 September and thereby to leave the path of war. Naturally one can find 100 reasons for this change of course . . . Two factors were probably decisive: (a) His observation that our people regarded the approach of war with a silent obstructiveness and were far from enthusiastic . . . and (b) Mussolini's appeal at the last moment, i.e. on the morning of the 28th, when the mobilisation was planned for 2.00 p.m. 20

Nazism, 1919–1945, ed. J. Noakes and G. Pridham, vol. III, 1988, pp. 720–21

Chamberlain, whose popularity soared briefly in Germany, as well as in Britain, defended the Munich Agreement in the House of Commons in these terms:

5.10   Chamberlain's speech in the House of Commons, 4 October 1938

The real triumph is that it has shown that representatives of four great powers can find it possible to agree on a way of carrying out a difficult and delicate operation by discussion instead of by force, and thereby they have averted a catastrophe which would have ended civilisation as we know it.

M. Gilbert, *Winston S. Churchill*, vol. V, 1976, pp. 992–3

The Munich Agreement was not the end of the story; nor was it ever intended to be. On 21 October Hitler gave the *Wehrmacht* a new directive which contained the following statement:

5.11

2   Liquidation of the remainder of the Czech State

It must be possible to smash at any time the remainder of the Czech State should it pursue an anti-German policy.

Nazism, 1919–1945, ed. J. Noakes and G. Pridham, vol. III, 1988, p. 724

Hitler exploited Slovak as he had Sudeten disaffection. He encouraged the Slovakian government to claim independence and then used the disintegration of Czechoslovakia as an excuse to invade it. On 14 March German troops entered the country. Bohemia was annexed to the Reich while Slovakia enjoyed a shadowy independence.

Questions

1 Was Chamberlain justified *on the basis of what he knew at the time* in concluding the Munich Agreement with Hitler?
2 Would you regard Weizsäcker's diary [5.9] as giving a reliable explanation for Hitler's conduct at Bad Godesburg?
3 'At Munich we lost a unique opportunity of easily and swiftly winning a war that was in any case inevitable' (Hitler to Martin Bormann in February 1945). What light does this comment throw (a) on Hitler's intentions in 1938 and (b) on the justification for the Munich Agreement?

We now enter what is perhaps the most controversial phase of Hitler's foreign policy: the making of the Nazi–Soviet Pact and the declaration of war on Poland. Grievances against Poland, stemming from the Treaty of Versailles, were firstly the loss of the Polish corridor, which now separated East Prussia from the rest of Germany, and secondly the status of Danzig, which had become an international port under the control of the League of Nations, despite its largely German population. Ribbentrop first broached proposals to the Polish ambassador, Lipski, on 24 October 1938. He suggested the incorporation of Danzig within the Reich, the construction of extra-territorial road and rail links between Germany and East Prussia, and Poland's accession to the Anti-Comintern Pact. These proposals were made again in January 1939 when Colonel Beck, the Foreign Minister, visited Berlin. At a meeting to consider them the Polish government, including the President, Vice Premier, Commander-in-Chief and Beck, it was concluded that:

5.12

If the Germans would maintain pressure in matters that are so secondary for them as Danzig and the highways, one could not have any illusions that we are threatened with large-scale conflict. These [German] objectives are only a pretext, and in view of that, a vacillating position on our side would lead us inevitably towards a slide, ending with the loss of independence and the role of Germany's vassal.

'The Origins of the Second World War' Reconsidered, ed. G. Martel, 1986, p. 196

Following the invasion of Czechoslovakia on 15 March 1939, Britain abandoned the policy of appeasement and on 31 March Chamberlain announced in the House of Commons that Britain would now guarantee Poland's independence. Fearing that this would only strengthen Polish intransigence, on 3 April Hitler ordered the initiation of military preparations against Poland, which were given the codename OPERATION WHITE:

5.13

German relations with Poland continue to be based on the principles of avoiding any disturbances. Should Poland, however, change her policy towards Germany, a final settlement might become necessary in spite of the Treaty in force with Poland.

    The aim then will be to destroy Polish military strength, and create in the East a situation which satisfies the requirements of national defence. The Free State of   5
Danzig will be proclaimed a part of the Reich territory at the outbreak of hostilities . . .

Nazism, 1919–1945, ed. J. Noakes and G. Pridham, vol. III, 1988, p. 735

On 22 May the Rome–Berlin Axis was transformed into a formal alliance, the so-called 'Pact of Steel', and it may be that it was this assurance that persuaded Hitler to go a step further in his preparations for a war with Poland. At a meeting with his commanders held on 23 May Hitler in a lengthy speech made the following pronouncements:

5.14

At present we are in a state of national ebullience as are two other states; Italy and Japan . . .

    It is not Danzig that is at stake. For us it is a matter of expanding our living space in the East and making food supplies secure and also solving the problem of the Baltic States . . .   5

    The problem of 'Poland' cannot be dissociated from the showdown with the West. Poland's internal solidarity against Bolshevism is doubtful. Therefore Poland is also a doubtful barrier against Russia.

    Success in war with the West with a rapid decision is questionable and so is Poland's attitude.   10

    The Polish regime will not stand up to Russian pressure. Poland sees danger in a German victory over the West and will try to deprive us of victory.

    There is therefore no question of sparing Poland and we are left with the decision:

To attack Poland at the first possible opportunity.   15
We cannot expect a repetition of Czechia. There will be war. Our task is to isolate Poland. Success in isolating her will be decisive.

    Therefore the Führer must reserve to himself the final order to strike. It must not come to a simultaneous showdown with the West (France and England).

    If it is not definitely certain that a German–Polish conflict will not lead to war   20
with the West, then the fight must be primarily against England and France.

    Thesis: Conflict with Poland – beginning with an attack on Poland – will only be successful if the West keeps out of the ring.

Nazism, 1919–1945, ed. J. Noakes and G. Pridham, vol. III, 1988, pp. 736–7

Having decided that war with Poland was inevitable, it was vital to ensure the neutrality of the Soviet Union. At the same time Britain and France were pressing for a Russian Alliance. The Russians continued to doubt the good faith of the British and French negotiators; their doubts were reinforced by the publication on 22 July in the British press of news of a draft economic agreement with Germany. This had been suggested by Helmut Wohltat, Deputy Director of Göring's Four Year Plan Organisation. On 24 July Chamberlain denied that any such agreement was under consideration, but the Russians refused to believe him. They were similarly unimpressed by what they considered to be the low calibre of the military mission sent to concert military operations, which arrived in Moscow on 11 August. Poland, as suspicious of Russia as she was of Germany, refused under any circumstances to allow the transit of Russian troops through her territory in the event of a war between Russia and Germany. This finally sabotaged the chances of any agreement between Russia and the Western democracies. Hitler had no such obstacles to contend with. Negotiations for an agreement with the USSR began at ambassadorial level in June 1939. Ribbentrop suggested that Germany might be in a good position to 'counteract any Japanese–Russian friction' (despite the Anti-Comintern Pact). As the deadline for war against Poland approached, Ribbentrop stepped up his overtures to Molotov, the Russian Foreign Minister. On 20 August Molotov sent the draft of a Non-Aggression Treaty to Berlin, and after a telegram from Hitler on 21 August agreed to receive Ribbentrop in Moscow on 23 August. The most authoritative record of what transpired is contained in the following account by a British historian:

5.15(a)

First they discussed the Soviet text of the Non-Aggression Pact as Ribbentrop had amended it in Königsberg. The magnificent preamble . . . went at once. After six years of shovelling mountains of cow-dung over each other, said Stalin (his language was much coarser), they could not suddenly go public with this kind of profession of eternal friendship. The rest of the text went easily. No aggression against each   5
other; no support for any third party attacking one or other of the signatories; continuous contact and exchanges of information; no membership of a grouping of powers 'aimed directly or indirectly' at the other; disputes to be settled by the 'friendly exchange of views'; duration for ten years; the pact to come into force on signature and not, as normal, when ratified.   10
   That was, of course, for public consumption. The real meat was contained in the secret protocol. Following on the clearest of statements made by Hitler and by Ribbentrop before his arrival, Stalin asked for a precisely defined division of spheres of influence. Poland was divided on the lines of the Rivers Narev, Vistula and San. The future of what might be left of Poland was to be settled by joint agreement.   15

Stalin expressed interest in the province of Bessarabia, with its large ethnic German minority, which Romania had annexed from a disintegrating Tsarist empire in 1918. Hitler wanted Lithuania and Latvia up to the Dvina River, including Riga. The rest of Latvia, Estonia and Finland went into Stalin's zone. Here Stalin's deep-rooted suspicion and fear of a Baltic invasion resurfaced. On the pretence that the Red Battle Fleet wanted Baltic harbours that would be ice-free all year round, he demanded all of Latvia . . . Ribbentrop had a free hand from Hitler, but not that free. This needed Hitler's agreement.

At 6 p.m. Ribbentrop returned to the German Embassy, bubbling over with enthusiasm . . . nothing had struck him as fake or unusual in the atmosphere. He was full of admiration for the clarity and directness with which Stalin and Molotov had spoken. A telegram, phoned in code to Berlin, obtained within three hours by the same means the Führer's permission to concede all Latvia . . .

As they broke up, around 2 a.m. on August 24, Stalin addressed his last words to Ribbentrop. The Soviet Union, he said, took the new pact very seriously. He could guarantee his word of honour that the Soviet Union would not betray Germany. Ribbentrop's reply is not recorded; which is perhaps just as well.

D.C. Watt, *How War Came*, 1989, pp. 458–61

The secret protocol to the Nazi–Soviet Pact took effect on 17 September 1939; Russian troops invaded Poland from the east to meet up with the invading German forces from the west. A British cartoonist made the following comment:

5.15(b) 'Rendezvous', a British comment on the Nazi–Soviet Pact

David Low, *Evening Standard*, 20 September 1939

Hitler anticipated the signature of the Pact and on 22 August he let his commanders into the secret at Obersalzburg. Admiral Canaris made notes on what Hitler said on this occasion. Hitler concluded:

5.16

The destruction of Poland has priority. The aim is to eliminate active forces, not to reach a definite line. Even if war breaks out in the West, the destruction of Poland remains the priority. A quick decision in view of the season.

I shall give a propagandist reason for starting the war, no matter whether it is plausible or not. [In fact German criminals, dressed in Polish uniforms, were   5
'found' outside a German radio station on the Polish border on 1 September.] The victor will not be asked whether he told the truth or not. When starting a war it is not right that matters, but victory.

Nazism, 1919–1945, ed. J. Noakes and G. Pridham, vol. III, 1988, p. 743

On 23 August Hitler gave instructions for the invasion of Poland to begin at 4.30 a.m. on 26 August. Two things caused him to countermand the order. On 25 August Britain ratified the Anglo-Polish Agreement of 31 March and Mussolini informed Hitler that Italy was not ready to fight. That afternoon Hitler postponed the attack. But on 26 August he again ordered the invasion to take place, this time on 1 September. The intervening delay of five days can be interpreted as a final attempt on Hitler's part either to secure a compromise or to split Britain and France from Poland, or simply as a loss of nerve on Hitler's part. According to A.J.P. Taylor, war broke out because Hitler launched 'on 29 August a diplomatic manoeuvre which he ought to have launched on 28 August' (*Origins of the Second World War*, 1964, p. 336).

The manoeuvre in question was an offer on Hitler's part to negotiate directly with the Poles, provided that a plenipotentiary arrived in Berlin within twenty-four hours. The Poles refused to be coerced, and on this occasion neither Britain nor France (unlike the case of Czechoslovakia) were prepared to abandon Poland. With his generals pressing for a decision, Hitler could afford to wait no longer, and on 1 September Poland was invaded. On 3 September, somewhat to Hitler's dismay, Britain and France declared war on Germany. Two comments on Hitler's real intentions and calculations in the summer of 1939 have come to light since the war. On 11 August he summoned Carl Burckhardt, League of Nations Commissioner for Danzig, to the Obersalzburg. In the course of a rambling, and at times emotional tirade, Hitler evidently said:

5.17

Everything I undertake is directed against the Russians; if the West is too stupid and blind to grasp this, then I shall be compelled to come to an agreement with the Russians, beat the West, and then after their defeat turn against the Soviet Union with all my forces. I need the Ukraine so they can't starve us out like in the last war.

C.J. Burckhardt, *Meine Danziger Mission, 1937–1939*, Munich, 1962

Albert Speer, who was in Berlin with Hitler in the final days before war was declared, gives this view of Hitler's state of mind:

5.18

Notes on the Polish crisis were exchanged with England. Out of the rush of events I particularly remember one evening in the conservatory of the Chancellor's residence. I had the impression that Hitler looked exhausted from overwork. He spoke with deep conviction to his intimate circle: 'This time the mistake of 1914 will not be repeated. Everything depends on making the other side accept responsibility. 5 In 1914 that was handled clumsily. And now again the ideas of the Foreign Office are simply useless. The best thing is for me to compose the notes myself.' . . .

When, on September 3, the Western powers followed up their ultimatum with declarations of war, Hitler was initially stunned, but quickly reassured himself and us by saying that England and France had obviously declared war merely as a sham, 10 in order not to lose face before the whole world. In spite of the declarations there would be no fighting; he was convinced of that, he said. He therefore ordered the *Wehrmacht* to remain strictly on the defensive. He felt that this decision of his showed remarkable acumen.

A. Speer, *Inside the Third Reich*, 1970, pp. 164–5

Questions

1 Does the evidence contained in 5.13 and 5.14 suggest that the Poles correctly interpreted Hitler's proposals on Danzig and the Polish Corridor [5.12]?
2 In the light of 5.15(a), 5.16 and 5.17, what led Hitler and Stalin to sign the Nazi–Soviet Pact? Is 5.15(b) an apposite comment on their motives?
3 To what extent do 5.14, 5.17 and 5.18 suggest that Hitler invaded Poland on the assumption that Britain and France would not intervene? Was he justified in making such an assumption?

4 How valuable is the testimony of Burckhardt and Speer as a guide to Hitler's state of mind in 1939 [3.17 and 3.18]?

5 'In the end the war was Hitler's war. It was not, perhaps, the war he wanted. But it was the war he was prepared to risk. Nothing could deter him' (D.C. Watt, *How War Came*, 1989). Do you agree?

Responsibility for the extension of the war

With the defeat of Poland in September 1939, Denmark and Norway in April 1940 and France in June 1940, Hitler had apparently accomplished all his objectives. This is evidently what he felt at the time. On 25 June 1940, three days after the Armistice with France, Hitler reflected:

5.19

The war in the west has ended. France has been conquered, and I shall come, in the shortest possible time, to an understanding with England. There still remains the conflict in the East. That, however, is a task which throws up world-wide problems, like the relationship with Japan and the distribution of power in the Pacific, one might perhaps tackle it in ten years' time, perhaps I shall leave it to my successor.   5
Now we have our hands full for years to come to digest and to consolidate what we have gained in Europe.

H.W. Koch, 'Hitler's "Programme" and the Genesis of Operation "Barbarossa"', *Aspects of the Third Reich*, 1985, p. 291

But Britain remained undefeated and refused the terms Hitler offered (in effect a free hand to Germany in Eastern Europe). The threats posed by Bolshevik Russia and international Jewry, illusory though they might be, had still to be tackled. Russia had occupied all the Baltic states in September 1939, including Lithuania, an arrangement that was unwillingly accepted by Hitler in return for minor concessions in Russian-occupied Poland. In December 1939 Stalin invaded Finland, and though Soviet troops were withdrawn in March 1940 it was now part of the Soviet sphere of influence. In the summer of 1940 Russia also laid claim to Bessarabia (part of Romania), and dangerously close to the oil wells on which Germany depended.

Two alternative strategies were pursued in the autumn of 1940. Ribbentrop urged the construction of a vast anti-British alliance which Spain, the Balkan countries, Japan and the Soviet Union would be invited to join. Alternatively, the defeat of Britain might be postponed and the search for *Lebensraum* in the East renewed. Linking the two strategies was the growing conviction that

British resistance was only kept alive by the prospect of Russian support (the 'continental sword'), and that one way of defeating Britain would be to defeat Russia first.

Hitler evidently veered between these two strategies, only finally committing himself to an attack on Russia in December 1940. 5.20–5.23 illustrate these uncertainties.

As early as 28 June 1940, the day Hitler had toured Paris, Speer overheard this conversation:

5.20

'Now we have shown what we are capable of,' Hitler was saying. 'Believe me, Keitel, a campaign against Russia would be like a child's game in a sandbox by comparison.'

A. Speer, *Inside the Third Reich*, 1970, p. 173

On 21 July 1940 Hitler had an interview with von Brauchitsch, Commander in Chief of the Army, whose conclusions were recorded by General Halder, his Chief of Staff. Among the possibilities considered were these:

5.21

8 Deal with Russian problem. Prepare ideas for it. The Führer has been informed.
(a) Build-up of German forces will take 4–6 weeks.
(b) Aim to defeat Russian army or at least seize as much Russian territory as is necessary to prevent air attacks on Berlin and Silesian industrial area . . .
(c) Political goal: Ukrainian empire

                          Baltic confederation
                          White Russia–Finland
                          Baltic states as a 'thorn in the flesh' [of Russia]

5

Nazism, 1919–1945, ed. J. Noakes and G. Pridham, vol. III, 1988, p. 788

A week later, the army commanders had evidently had second thoughts. This time Halder recorded the recommendations of another conference:

5.22

(d) In the event of our being unable to force a decision on England and of the danger of England allying herself with Russia, the answer to the question of whether one should launch a two front war against Russia is that it is better to keep on friendly terms with Russia. A visit to Stalin would be desirable. Russia's aspirations toward the Straits and in the direction of the Persian Gulf need not worry us . . .

Nazism, 1919–1945, ed. J. Noakes and G. Pridham, vol. III, 1988, p. 789

In the meantime Ribbentrop had been urging Japanese co-operation in transforming the international triangle (Germany, Italy and Japan) into an international square, by the addition of the Soviet Union. He held out the following prospect to the former Japanese Foreign Minister, Sato, who visited Berlin in September 1940:

5.23

Under the new world order, Japan would hold sway in Eastern Asia, Russia in Asia itself, Germany and Italy in Europe; and also in Africa it would be exclusively Germany and Italy, perhaps with a few other interested nations, who would gain ascendancy and rule.

W. Michalka, *Aspects of the Third Reich*, ed. H.W. Koch, 1985, p. 281

As a first step to this objective the Three Power Pact between Germany, Italy and Japan was signed on 27 September 1940. Russia was told about the Pact on 25 September, though not consulted. The ambivalence of German policy is well illustrated in Directive Number 18, given to Halder by Hitler on 12 November 1940:

5.24

5 Russia

Political discussions have been initiated with the aim of clarifying Russia's attitude for the coming period. Regardless of what results those discussions will have, all preparations for the East which have been orally ordered, are to be continued.

Directives on this will follow as soon as the outline of the Army's plan of operations is submitted to, and approved by, me.

Nazism, 1919–1945, ed. J. Noakes and G. Pridham, vol. III, 1988, p. 800

The political discussions referred to above were the talks which Molotov had with Hitler and Ribbentrop on 12 and 13 November. Hitler and Ribbentrop tried to secure Russia's adhesion to the Three Power Pact, but Molotov wanted detailed assurances about Russian claims to Finland and the Baltic states and recognition of Soviet interests in the Balkans. The talks ended inconclusively.

What evidently turned the scales were the specific demands submitted by Molotov on his return to Russia as conditions for joining the Three Power Pact:

5.25

Russia made her joining the tripartite pact conditional on the withdrawal of all
German forces from Finnish soil. All economic obligations towards Germany by
Finland would be assumed by Russia. Furthermore, Russia insisted on bases for
land and naval forces at the Bosphorus and the Dardanelles. Thirdly the Kremlin
demanded Germany's recognition of Russian claims to the territory south of Baku   5
and Batum in the direction of the Persian Gulf. Lastly Japan would have to cede to
Russia its concessions for the exploitation of oil and coal resources in North
Sakhalin. And last but not least, Moscow demanded the abrogation of the Russo-
German treaties. Hitler read the note, put it in his desk and did not bother to reply.
The dice had been cast.

H.W. Koch, 'Hitler's "Programme" and the Genesis of Operation
"Barbarossa"', *Aspects of the Third Reich*, 1985, p. 319

5.26   An alternative view from Robert Cecil

It is, of course, clear that Hitler would not have acceded to such terms except under
duress. It will become equally clear, as the narrative proceeds, that Stalin had no
intention of confronting Hitler with such a stark alternative; indeed as German
silence persisted, the Russians showed themselves increasingly anxious to avert a
recourse to arms. Subsequently, Hitler liked to tell his Generals, as for example   5
Guderian, that it was Molotov's visit that made him feel that war was inevitable; but
this conclusion would only have been justified if Stalin, failing to extract a reply to
the Russian note, had begun to mobilise. Instead it was the Germans who were
covertly mobilising their forces in the East. The whole negotiation had been 'a
blind'.

R. Cecil, *Hitler's Decision to Invade Russia*, 1975, pp. 109–10

Whatever Hitler's reasons, on 5 December a conference was held at which
detailed plans for the invasion of Russia were considered, and on 18 December
Hitler issued a military directive, Operation Barbarossa, calling for preparations to be completed by 18 May. On 21 June, the day before it was
launched, Hitler explained his reasoning in a letter to Mussolini:

5.27

The situation: England has lost this war. With the right of the drowning person, she
grasps at every straw which, in her imagination, might serve as a sheet anchor.
Nevertheless, some of her hopes are naturally not without a certain logic. England
has thus far always conducted her wars with help from the Continent. The
destruction of France – in fact the elimination of all West European positions – is   5

directing the glances of the British warmongers continually to the place from which they tried to start the war: to Soviet Russia . . .

The concentration of Russian forces – I had General Jodl submit the most recent to your Attaché here, General Marras – is tremendous. Really, all available Russian forces are at our border.   10

The situation in England itself is bad; the provision of food and raw materials is growing steadily more difficult. The martial spirit to make war, after all, lives only on hopes. These hopes are based solely on two asumptions: Russia and America. We have no chance of eliminating America. But it does lie in our power to exclude Russia. The elimination of Russia means, at the same time, a tremendous relief for   15 Japan in East Asia, and thereby the possibility of a much stronger threat to American activities through Japanese intervention . . .

In conclusion, let me say one thing more, Duce. Since I struggled through to this decision, I again feel spiritually free. The partnership with the Soviet Union, in spite of the complete sincerity of the efforts to bring about a final conciliation, was   20 nevertheless often very irksome for me, for in some way or other it seemed to be a break with my whole origin, my concepts, and my former obligations. I am happy now to be relieved of these mental agonies. With hearty and comradely greetings,

Yours,
Adolf Hitler.

Nazism, 1919–1945, ed. J. Noakes and G. Pridham, vol. III, 1988, pp. 815–17

Questions

1 How do you account for the uncertainty of German policy in the autumn of 1940 [5.19–5.24]?
2 Was Hitler launching a preventative war, or a war of territorial aggrandisement when he attacked Russia in June 1941 [5.25–5.27]?
3 Examine the relevance of *Mein Kampf* [2.10(f)] as an explanation of Hitler's decision to invade Russia.
4 Which of the explanations [5.25, 5.26] for the breakdown of the Nazi–Soviet Pact do you find the more convincing, and why?

6 Responses to Nazi rule

One of the characteristic features of Nazi ideology was its belief that all must be made to conform to the norms of the regime, a process that has been summed up in the term *Gleichschaltung*, literally 'forcing into line'. The process of *Gleichschaltung* was applied to political parties, the civil service and trade unions in 1933. It was extended to the press and radio shortly after [6.2]. Schools and universities were also brought under Nazi control. By 1937, 97 per cent of all schoolteachers were members of the National Socialist Teachers' League. Universities were purged of Jews and all those whose political reliability was in doubt. 1,145 academic staff (15 per cent of the total) were removed in 1933–34 alone. The Hitler Youth movement, and its female equivalent, the *Bund Deutscher Madel* (League of German Maidens), were the only permitted youth organisations after 1936, and membership was made compulsory in 1939 for all between the ages of ten and eighteen. By 1939 the Nazi regime had extended its control over almost every social, professional and economic organisation and institution.

Two strategies were employed to achieve this objective: propaganda and terror. From 1933 onwards the German public was fed a diet of carefully processed information all designed to stress the virtues of the Führer and the success of his rule. At the same time the slightest overt expression of dissent, let alone organised opposition, was liable to be met by arrest and imprisonment at best, execution at worst. In assessing German responses to the crimes of Hitler's regime this needs to be remembered. The following documents show both strategies at work.

6.1 The role of propaganda

Every movement will first have to sift the human material it wins into two large groups; supporters and members.

The function of propaganda is to attract supporters, the function of organisation to win members. Being a supporter is rooted only in understanding, membership is the courage personally to advocate and disseminate what has been understood.

Understanding in its passive form corresponds to the majority of mankind which is lazy and cowardly. Membership requires an activistic frame of mind and this corresponds only to the minority of men. . .

5

Propaganda works on the general public from the standpoint of an idea and makes them ripe for the victory of this idea, while the organisation achieves victory   10 by the persistent, organic, and militant union of those supporters who seem willing and able to carry on the fight for victory.

A. Hitler, *Mein Kampf*, translated by Ralph Manheim, 1969, pp. 529–30

In line with the importance which Hitler attached to propaganda, one of his first actions as Chancellor, after the election victory of March 1933, was to appoint Goebbels to the cabinet as Minister for Information and Propaganda. Goebbels' understanding of his role is well indicated in the instruction he gave to the Controllers of German Radio on 25 March 1933:

6.2

We make no bones about the fact that the radio belongs to us and to no one else, And we will place the radio in the service of our ideology [*Idee*] and [the speaker bangs on the lectern] no other ideology will find expression here . . . The radio must subordinate itself to the goals which the Government of the national revolution has set itself. The Government will give the necessary instructions . . .

Nazism, 1919–1945, ed. J. Noakes and G. Pridham, vol. II, 1984, p. 385

But Goebbels was too subtle a propagandist simply to repress hostile opinions. He encouraged positive support of the regime by stressing the virtues of Nazism, as in the literature given to the building of *Autobahns*, under the Battle for Work programme inaugurated by Hitler in March 1934 [6.3(a)] and in the publicity associated with it [6.3(b)].

6.3(a)   Song in celebration of work

God bless work and our beginning,
God bless the Führer and this time
Stand at our side while we reclaim the land.
Make us ready at every hour,
To serve Germany with all our hearts.   5

God bless work and all our efforts,
God bless the spades with shining gleam.
May the work of our hands bring such success
That every spadeful we turn shall be
A prayer for Germany.

Dienst unterm Spaten, Central Publishing Company of the *NSDAP*, Munich, 1937, p. 9

6.3(b)   Hitler digging the *Autobahn*

Agentur Weltbild GmbH, Ullstein

Questions

1 Examine the distinction which Hitler makes between members and supporters of a movement [6.1]. What view does he take of supporters?
2 What, according to Hitler and Goebbels, is the function of propaganda? Need it bear any relation to truth [6.1, 6.2]?
3 What message was 6.3(b) intended to convey?
4 What virtues are commended in 6.3(a)? Is there anything to which you would take exception in this document?

The other side of the coin to the *Volksgemeinschaft* (sense of community) which Nazism encouraged was its unremitting hostility to any sign of dissent. The Law of 28 February 1933 removing individual rights was never repealed, despite Hitler's protestations at the time. Instead its range was extended by two decrees passed on 21 March 1933 and 10 December 1934 [6.4]. The Security Services were greatly expanded. The *SS* (*Schutzstaffel*, Defence Unit) set up in 1925, had 52,000 members by 1933. The *SS* also had its own Security Service (*Sicherheitsdienst, SD*) set up by Heydrich in 1931. In Prussia, Göring created the *Geheime Staatspolizei* (*Gestapo*) when he took over as Minister. As might have been expected there was initially a polycratic struggle for power between these various forces, but in this case a degree of centralisation was achieved. Himmler became Inspector of the *Gestapo* in 1934 and was made *Reichsführer SS* and Chief of Police in 1936. In 1939 the *Reichssicherheitshauptamt* (*RSHA* – The Reich Central Bureau for Security) was set up under Himmler's direction, and this organisation exercised a very tight control over all security questions, including, later on, responsibility for anti-Semitic policies.

The Police, of whatever branch, were encouraged to clamp down on any sign of opposition [6.5]. The device of 'protective custody' could be, and was, employed to detain suspects at will [6.6]; and the Security Services showed scant respect for such laws as did protect the rights of the individual [6.7]. It has been calculated that 150,000 men and women were detained in concentration camps between 1933 and 1939, and in 1939, before the outbreak of war, there were 25,000 detainees. A recent estimate suggests that as many as 3 million Germans saw the inside of a concentration camp or prison between 1933 and 1945, while as many as 32,500 Germans may have been executed for political reasons over the same period (M. Balfour, *Withstanding Hitler's Germany, 1933–45*, 1988, pp. 255–58). 6.4–6.7 give substance to these figures.

6.4   Decree for the Protection of the Nationalist Movement against Malicious Attacks upon the Government, 21 March 1933

Paragraph 3

1 Whoever purposely makes or circulates a statement of a factual nature which is grossly exaggerated or which may seriously harm the welfare of the Reich . . . or the reputation of the National Government . . . is to be punished, providing that no more severe punishment is decreed in other regulations, with imprisonment of up to   5 two years and, if he makes or spreads the statement publicly, with imprisonment of not less than three months.

Nazism, 1919–1945, ed. J. Noakes and G. Pridham, vol. II, 1984, p. 478

6.5   Police instructions

Measures against immorality and hostility towards the State

In accordance with §14 of the police administration law which states that the police force is obliged to protect the State from dangers to public law and order, the Deutsche Polizei Beamter, the official organ of the *Kameradschaftsbund*, outlines rules and regulations which are also of importance when dealing with the general   5
public.

For example those who, on festive occasions, deliberately decline from observing the Hitler salute whilst singing the Horst Wessel song [Horst Wessel was an *SA* man killed in a fight with Communists in 1930] manifest hostility towards the State. If the refusal to observe the usual German greeting [*Heil Hitler!*] towards civil   10
servants or the administrative authority, is deliberate and manifests disrespect, it must be regarded as a danger to public security.

Concentration Camp Dachau, Catalogue, *Comité International de Dachau,* **Munich, 1978, p. 39**

6.6   Protective custody

Secret State Police **Secret State Police Office** **IV G 2 Nr.F8833**	Berlin SW 11, April 13, 1942 Prince Albertstr. 8

PROTECTIVE CUSTODY ORDER

Christian name and surname	Johannes Flintrop
Date and Place of Birth	May 23, 1904-Wuppertal
Occupation	Chaplain
Status	Single
Nationality	German
Race (in case of non-Aryans)	
Domicile:	Lettman, Schlageterstr. 21

is to be taken into protective custody

Reasons:
State Police evidence shows that his/her behaviour constitutes a danger to the existence and security of people and State because:
Ignoring an earlier police complaint regarding his detrimental attitude towards the State he has abused his clerical position to make defeatist remarks to create unrest and commotion which could serve to shake the German People's faith in the ultimate victory and unfailing strength of our armed forces.

[Flintrop died on 17 August 1942 in Dachau, supposedly of 'phlegmone of the left foot', brought on by malnutrition.]

Concentration Camp Dachau, Catalogue, *Comité International de Dachau,* **Munich, 1978, pp. 55–6**

6.7   A speech by Himmler to the Committee for Police Law of the Academy of German Law in 1936

[Himmler begins by complaining that under the Weimar Republic whenever police officers arrested a criminal they had to watch out that they did not get into trouble themselves while the criminal got away scot-free.] We National Socialists then set to work – it may sound odd that I should say this in the Academy of German Law – but you will understand what I mean – not without justice behind us since we had   5
that within ourselves, but possibly outside the law. Right from the start I took the view that it did not matter in the least if our actions were contrary to some clause in the law; in my work for the Führer and the nation, I do what my conscience and common sense tell me is right . . .

Nazism, 1919–1945, ed. J. Noakes and G. Pridham, vol. II, 1984, pp. 505–6

Questions

1 What do **6.4** and **6.5** imply about the popularity of Hitler's regime? How reliable are they as sources of evidence?
2 What were Himmler's conceptions of law and justice [**6.7**]?
3 What is the significance of the phrase 'State Police evidence shows that his/ her behaviour constitutes a danger to the existence and security of people and state because' [**6.6**]?
4 From the evidence of **6.6** and **6.7**, what protection from arrest did any German citizen have under the Third Reich?

In the climate of opinion created both by ceaseless propaganda and constant surveillance, Germans responded in countless different ways to Hitler's policies. We need also to remember that the years 1933–45 were among the most dynamic in German history. During them Germany passed from political disorder and economic depression to domestic peace and relative prosperity; by the end of 1939 all the discriminatory clauses of the Treaty of Versailles had been removed and the borders of the Reich extended into Czechoslovakia and western Poland; by the summer of 1940 the whole of western Europe apart from Britain was under German domination. But by 1944 many of Germany's cities were smoking ruins, Russian troops were poised on her eastern borders and the Allies were about to invade France. It would be surprising if the measure of support for Hitler did not rise and fall with these changes in German fortunes, and in the majority of cases this is probably what happened. Not only was there a wide spectrum of responses to Hitler, ranging from enthusiastic support through willing or unwilling aquiescence to outright hostility, the composition of this spectrum alters over time as scepticism gives way first to approval and then to disillusion.

As a way of measuring these responses we will look first at the evidence for Hitler's popularity with the acquiescent majority. Then we examine the attitudes of Hitler's most committed supporters, in connection with the worst of his crimes. The chapter ends with a survey of Hitler's opponents.

The acquiescent majority

Recent commentators have stressed the popularity of Hitler's regime.

6.8   A public opinion survey conducted in 1951

As late as 1951 almost half of those citizens of the Federal Republic of Germany questioned in a public opinion survey described the period between 1933 and 1939 as the one in which things had gone best for Germany.

Ulrich Herbert, 'Good Times, Bad Times: Memories of the Third Reich', *Life in the Third Reich*, ed. R. Bessel, 1987, p. 97

6.9   A speech by a prominent member of the Christian Democratic party, Philip Jenninger, then Speaker of the *Bundestag* (the West German Parliament), 11 November 1988

The re-incorporation of the Saar, the introduction of the general draft, massive rearmament, the conclusion of the German–British fleet accords, the Olympic summer games in Berlin, the annexation of Austria, the Great German Empire and finally, the Munich agreement, the cutting up of Czechoslovakia – the Versailles Accord was really just a scrap of paper and the German Empire was the leading   5
power.

For the Germans who saw the Weimar Republic mainly as a consequence of foreign policy humiliations, all this must have seemed a miracle. And not only that; mass unemployment turned into full employment, from mass misery there was something like prosperity for the widest sections (of the population). Instead of   10
desperation and hopelessness, optimism and self-confidence reigned. Didn't Hitler just make reality what was just a promise under Wilhelm II, that is to bring wonderful times for the Germans?

The *Guardian*, 12 November 1988

As **6.8** and **6.9** would seem to suggest, Hitler certainly commanded a good deal of voluntary support. Ian Kershaw has suggested seven reasons for the success of the Hitler myth. He was seen as the bringer of strong rule and the restorer of public morality; he championed national rather than selfish class interests. He was the architect of Germany's economic miracle which had ended unemployment and brought prosperity. He was a moderating influence on the extremists within his party. He was fanatically committed in his opposition to the enemies of the people, Bolsheviks and Jews in particular, though his anti-Semitism was played down when it suited him. He was successfully, if inaccurately, portrayed as a man of peace until 1939, and as a brilliant strategist thereafter (Ian Kershaw, 'Hitler and the Germans', *Life in the Third Reich*, ed. R. Bessell, 1987, pp. 47–53).

In order to assess what proportion of the general public shared a belief in this mythology of Hitler, two kinds of evidence have been assembled. Though no public opinion polls were held during the Nazi era, Hitler did have plebiscites on a number of issues with which he was personally identified, and there were elections to the *Reichstag* in 1934 and 1936. Three of these occasions have been selected [6.10]. Their results need to be read in the light of the comments on how the plebiscites were conducted in 6.11 and 6.12.

Plebiscites

6.10(a)   12 November 1933, on the decision to leave the League of Nations

Entitled to vote	Votes cast	%	Yes	%	No	%	Invalid votes
45,176,713	43,491,575	96.3	40,632,628	95.1	2,101,191	4.9	750,270

6.10(b)   Elections to the *Reichstag*, 29 March 1936 (also coupled with vote to approve the Remilitarisation of the Rhineland)

Total of qualified voters	45,453,691
Total of votes cast	45,001,489 = 99%
Votes cast against the list and votes invalid	542,211
For the list of Nazi candidates	44,461,278 = 98.8%

6.10(c)   Plebiscite to approve the *Anschluss* with Austria, 10 April 1938

Yes: 48,799,269 out of 49,646,950 voters = 99.08%

Norman H. Baynes (ed.), *The Speeches of Adolf Hitler*, vol. II, 1942, pp. 1143, 1321, 1459

Bernt Engelmann was a schoolboy of twelve in 1933. He has based his book, *In Hitler's Germany*, on his own experiences, and on interviews conducted since with those who lived through the period.

6.11   A comment on the 1936 election to the *Reichstag*

Three weeks later [after the Remilitarisation of the Rhineland], after unprecedented propaganda efforts, the Nazi leadership staged new 'elections'. The right to vote was declared an obligation to vote, and only the Nazi slate of candidates was presented. The ballot was cleverly tied to a referendum in which the voter had to indicate whether he or she supported 'the restoration of the German people's honour' as it   5
had been achieved by the Führer through the occupation of the Rhineland.

For this election the Nazi party and its many auxiliary organisations exerted more direct pressure on voters than ever before. In factories, tenants' organisations, offices, and even schools, the same slogans were heard over and over again for three weeks: 'No one must miss this election!' 'Every vote for the Führer!' 'Anyone who   10
does not vote for Hitler is a traitor to the Volk!'

On Sunday, March 29, 1936, shortly before midnight, Reich Propaganda Minister Goebbels triumphantly announced the election results: 'Ninety-nine per cent of all Germans have voted for Adolf Hitler and the NSDAP! No one in Germany was surprised. Everyone had felt the pressure; everyone knew about the   15
harassment, manipulation, and falsification at the police stations. An entire nation had bowed to a system of terror.

B. Engelmann, *In Hitler's Germany*, 1988, p. 95

6.12   A police report on the plebiscite of 10 April 1938

Copy of a schedule is attached herewith enumerating the persons who cast 'No' votes or invalid votes at Kappel, district of Simmern. The invalid votes are listed first, ending with –; thereafter come the 'No' votes.

The control was effected in the following way: some members of the election committee marked all the ballot papers with numbers. During the ballot itself, a   5
voters' list was made up. The ballot papers were handed out in numerical order, therefore it was possible with the aid of this list to find out the persons who cast 'No' votes or invalid votes. One sample of these marked ballot papers is enclosed. The marking was done on the back of ballot papers with skimmed milk.

The ballot cast by the Protestant parson Alfred Wolferts is also enclosed . . .

Nazism, 1919–1945, ed. J. Noakes and G. Pridham, vol. II, 1984, p. 595

Individual responses to Hitler

Another way of probing responses to Hitler is through the reactions of particular individuals. Four representative samples have been selected for this purpose, 6.13(a–d).

6.13(a)

'You've left out one category,' put in Grete, who had said nothing up to this point. 'There were also those who believed in the Führer as a saviour and were hypnotised by him. My mother, for example. She never got any benefit from being one of the earliest members of the Nazi Party and of the Nazi Women's League, or at least no material benefit. They let her sit in the front row at Nazi events, and once she   5
handed a bouquet to the Führer – that was the high point of her life . . . She was convinced everything the Nazis did was right and essential, and she dismissed all the whispers of atrocities as stupid, malicious gossip. But she never harmed anyone – she always wanted the best for people. In May of '45 her whole world collapsed. At the time – I was just sixteen – we had been evacuated to Fürstenfeldbruck.   10
Mother was among those the Americans forced to tour Dachau, and I had to go along. I'll never forget those heaps of emaciated corpses . . . Mother suffered a nervous breakdown. It took her a long time to recover.'

B. Engelmann, *In Hitler's Germany*, 1988, p. 34

Christabel Bielenberg, an Englishwoman married to a German lawyer, Peter Bielenberg, who joined the resistance to Hitler, recalls a conversation in the autumn of 1939 with her gardener in Berlin, Herr Neisse. He had lost his savings in 1923 and become unemployed in 1929. He had joined the party in 1931 and for his services was appointed the local *Blockwart* (warden), the lowest rung on the party ladder:

6.13(b)

For Herr Neisse, Hitler was a homely sincere man who had been a simple soldier like himself and whose sole extravagance was his passionate devotion to Germany and to Germany's well-being. 'He is a child-lover you see, Frau Dr, and dogs too.' *Schlicht*, modest, was the word Herr Neisse and I had agreed on to sum up our Leader's virtues in spite of the fact that I could have thought up an epithet or two   5
which would have filled the bill more accurately.

Christabel Bielenberg, *The Past is Myself*, 1984, p. 56

An oral history project carried out in the town of Essen between 1983 and 1987 produced two hundred life histories describing the experiences of industrial workers between 1930 and 1960. One such was Ernest Bromberg, born in 1905, who worked for the Krupp steel works. He described his involvement with Nazi political activities in the 1930s as follows:

6.13(c)

No time for it, when you're on three shift working – with the Labour Front, later on – oh God, yes – people kicked against it a bit and then just carried on, you know! Yes, well obviously, if you were on piece work, you didn't have any time to make speeches, you got up in the morning when you had to, you didn't overstretch your break periods – because after all – the money was tempting . . . I didn't worry any 5
more about the Nazis, put it that way, apart from my Labour Front contribution I just didn't have anything to do with the Nazis, you know, and anyway I was tied up with my Protestant clubs all week you know . . . Nothing really changed there.

Ulrich Herbert, 'Good Times, Bad Times: Memories of the Third Reich', *Life in the Third Reich*, **ed. R. Bessel, 1987, p. 97**

Our fourth example is taken from a cache of letters written by the wife of a Professor of English at Hamburg University, Mathilde Wolff-Monckeburg. She herself was the daughter of a prosperous Hamburg lawyer. Several of her children were living outside Germany when the war broke out and she kept a journal in the form of letters to them which were written but never posted. The letters were discovered by her daughter Ruth when going through her mother's possessions after her mother's death in 1978.

6.13(d)   September 1940

In truth this whole campaign had been planned long ago, the Führer's blind lust for conquest being the driving force behind the deed. For me nothing was more devastating than the fact that nobody stood up against this, but remained passive and weak. It was as if we were caught in a stranglehold. And, worst of all, one even gets used to being half throttled; what at first appeared to be unbearable pressures 5
become a habit easier to tolerate; hate and desperation are diluted with time.

Mathilde Wolff-Monckeberg, *On the Other Side, to My Children: from Germany, 1940–45*, **translated and edited by Ruth Evans, 1979, p. 28**

Questions

1 What differences can you detect between the plebiscite results recorded on 12 November 1933 and those on 29 March 1936? How would you account for them?

2 Do the comments made in **6.11** and **6.12** suggest that no credence should be given to plebiscites held under the Nazis as indicators of the popularity of Hitler and his policies?
3 For what qualities was Hitler admired in **6.13(a, b)**?
4 How do you account for the different perceptions of Hitler reflected in **6.13(a–d)**?
5 To what extent do you think that responses to Hitler were determined by class and education?

Committed supporters

Hitler's most devoted followers were drawn from the ranks of the *SS* and the upper echelons of the Nazi party. Whether from conviction or self-interest, they showed themselves willing to obey his every whim, and to carry out his orders to the letter. An awful but revealing testimony to this subordination is to be found in the treatment of the Jews which culminated in the holocaust. A great deal of controversy still surrounds the genesis of the decision to liquidate the Jewish people (see, for example, Gerald Fleming, *Hitler and the Final Solution*, 1982). But whether the policy of extermination was deliberately ordered by Hitler or whether it occurred partly 'as a way out of a blind alley into which the National Socialists had manoeuvred themselves' (M. Broszat, 'The Genesis of the Final Solution', *Aspects of the Third Reich*, ed. H.W. Koch, p. 391) matters less than the evident willingness of countless Germans to carry out what they, at any rate, took to be the *Führer*'s wishes.

Hitler made no bones about his wish to rid German soil of Jews, and on at least two occasions made public his belief that annihilation was a perfectly acceptable, indeed desirable, solution [**6.14**]. Various alternatives were canvassed: emigration to Palestine or, after the fall of France, to Madagascar. Jews might be settled in eastern Poland, or, if the Russian campaign succeeded, beyond the Urals. But Jews were being deliberately put to death on the invasion of Poland as early as 1939, and there seems little doubt that extermination was contemplated in June 1941, and became official policy in January 1942 at the Wannsee Conference [**6.16**].

It may be true that no written order with Hitler's signature on it ordering the annihilation of the Jewish people has been found. But Hitler frequently failed to sign directives and both Himmler and Heydrich, who bear most responsibility for implementing the final solution, were in no doubt that they were carrying out Hitler's express wishes [**6.17**]. How many Germans were also directly implicated is impossible to say, but certainly included were all those who staffed the concentration camps, the *Einsatzgruppen* (special *SS* action groups who accompanied the armies which invaded Poland and Russia) and probably those like Claus Barbie in France who rounded up non-German Jews and transported them to the extermination camps. 6.14–6.18 illustrate the parts played by some of those involved in the final solution.

6.14(a)   *Mein Kampf*

If, at the beginning of the war and during the war, twelve or fifteen thousand of these Hebrew corrupters of the people had been held under poison gas, as happened to hundreds of thousands of our best German brothers in the field, the sacrifice of millions at the front would not have been in vain.

Adolf Hitler, *Mein Kampf*, translated by Ralph Manheim, 1969, p. 620

6.14(b)   Hitler's speech to the *Reichstag*, 30 January 1939

. . . Today I will once more be a prophet: if the international Jewish financiers in and outside Europe should succeed in plunging the nations once more into a world war, then the result will be not the Bolshevising of the earth, and thus the victory of Jewry, but the annihilation of the Jewish race in Europe!

Nazism, 1919–1945, ed. J. Noakes and G. Pridham, vol. III, 1988, p. 1048

Following the invasion of Russia in June 1941 it has been estimated that the *Einsatzgruppen* were responsible for at least 700,000 Jewish deaths. Problems were also being encountered in feeding the Polish Jews who had concentrated into ghettoes. It is in this context that the following document needs to be read. It was signed by Göring, though drafted by Heydrich, Himmler's immediate subordinate:

6.15   Directive on the Jewish problem, 31 July 1941

To supplement the task that was assigned to you on 24 January 1939, which dealt with the Jewish problem by emigration and evacuation in the most suitable way, I hereby charge you with making all necessary preparations with regard to organisational, technical and material matters for bringing about a complete solution of the Jewish question within the German sphere of influence in Europe . . .

Nazism, 1919–1945, ed. J. Noakes and G. Pridham, vol. III, 1988, p. 1104

It was in pursuance of this order that Heydrich summoned a conference of interested parties to meet in Berlin on 29 November 1941. The meeting was postponed to 20 January 1942 and was held at the office of the International

Criminal Police Commission, Wannsee, Berlin (it was known subsequently as the Wannsee Conference). Fourteen people attended, including representatives from the *RSHA*, the Reich Chancellery, the Ministry of Justice, the Foreign Office, the Four Year Plan, those responsible for administering Poland, and the commander of the *SS* in Latvia, who had already cleared his area of Jews by gassing and shooting them. Adolf Eichmann of the *RSHA* took the minutes, which even in the expurgated account they give of the proceedings make chilling reading:

6.16

In pursuance of the final solution, the Jews will be conscripted for labour in the east under appropriate supervision. Large labour gangs will be formed from those fit for work, with the sexes separated, which will be sent to those areas for road construction and undoubtedly a large number of them will drop out through natural wastage. The remainder who survive – and they will certainly be those who have the   5
greatest powers of endurance – will have to be dealt with accordingly. For, if released, they would, as a natural selection of the fittest, form a germ cell from which the Jewish race could regenerate itself. (That is the lesson of history.)

   In the process of carrying out the final solution Europe will be combed through from west to east.

Nazism, 1919–1945, ed. J. Noakes and G. Pridham, vol. III, 1988, p. 1131

In subsequent interrogation by an Israeli court Eichmann admitted that 'the discussion covered killing, elimination and annihilation' (G. Fleming, *Hitler and the Final Solution*, 1986, p. 92).

   Three contrasting documents illustrate the final solution as it was seen by the men who ordered it and one of those whose task it was to carry it out.

6.17(a)   Himmler's speech to a group of *SS* generals, Posen, 4 October 1943

. . . I also want to talk to you quite frankly about a very grave matter . . . I am referring to the Jewish evacuation programme, the extermination of the Jewish people . . . Most of you will know what it means when a hundred corpses are lying side by side, or five hundred or a thousand are lying there. To have stuck it out and – apart from a few exceptions due to human weakness – to have remained decent,   5
that is what has made us tough. This is a glorious page in our history and one that has never been written and can never be written . . .

Nazism, 1919–1945, ed. J. Noakes and G. Pridham, vol. III, 1988, p. 1199

At another gathering of generals on 26 January 1944 in Posen, Himmler, according to the sworn testimony of an eye witness, Rudolf-Christoph Freiherr von Gersdorff, said in effect:

6.17(b)

When the Führer gave me the order to carry out the total solution of the Jewish question, I at first hesitated, uncertain whether I could demand of my worthy SS men the execution of such a horrid assignment . . . But this was ultimately a matter of a Führer order, and therefore I could have no misgivings. In the meantime, the assignment has been carried out and there is no longer a Jewish question.

G. Fleming, *Hitler and The Final Solution*, 1986, p. 53

Christabel Bielenberg describes an encounter with one who in his own way was also a victim of the final solution. The speaker is a Latvian whose country was invaded by Russia in 1939 and 'liberated' by Germany in 1941.

6.18

'Well, they told us that we could revenge ourselves on our enemies and they sent us to Poland. Not to fight the Poles, oh no, they had been defeated long ago – but to kill Jews. We just had the shooting to do, others did the burying,' he drew a deep, sighing breath. 'Do you know what it means – to kill Jews, men, women, and children as they stand in a semi-circle around the machine guns? I belonged to what 5 is called an *Einsatzkommando*, an extermination squad – so I know . . . and once when the circle stood around us, an old man stepped out of the ranks, he had long hair and a beard, a priest of some sort, I suppose. Anyway, he came towards us, slowly across the grass, slowly step by step, and within a few feet of the guns he stopped and looked at us one after another, a straight, deep, dark and terrible look. 10 "My children," he said, "God is watching what you do." He turned from us then, and someone shot him in the back before he had gone more than a few steps. But I – I could not forget that look, even now it burns into me.'

C. Bielenberg, *The Past is Myself*, 1984, pp. 251–2

Questions

1 On the basis of the evidence presented here [6.14–6.17], how much responsibility would you attribute to Hitler for the policy of liquidation of the Jews?
2 What can be inferred from the Minutes of the Wannsee Conference [6.16], and from those who attended it, about the extent to which knowledge of the planned annihilation of the Jews was shared by the German people?

3 Examine the differences in the way in which Himmler referred to the policies of extermination in **6.17(a)** and **6.17(b)**. How do you account for the changes?

4 What light do **6.15–6.18** throw on German willingness to participate in the extermination of the Jews?

Resistance to Hitler

Resistance to Hitler was fraught with difficulties from the outset. The pseudo-legal methods by which Hitler seized power made it difficult to identify the point at which legitimacy passed to illegality. Both the Centre and the Social Democratic parties were faced with this problem. Those who resisted Hitler were bitterly divided among themselves. The split between the Communists and the Social Democrats which had so weakened working-class opposition to Hitler before 1933 continued thereafter. Stalin's belated attempt to sponsor Popular Fronts in Europe in opposition to Fascism had little success in Germany, especially after the signature of the Nazi–Soviet Pact. Members of the Kreisau circle, a resistance group founded by Count Helmuth von Moltke, which met on his estate at Kreisau from 1940 onwards, were united in their opposition to Hitler. But right wingers such as Carl Goedeler, the ex-mayor of Leipzig, could not agree with Social Democrats such as Julius Leber on what to put in place of the Nazi regime.

But perhaps the worst problem faced by those who resisted Hitler was the dilemma posed by the Second World War. Dietrich Bonhoeffer, a Lutheran pastor who joined the resistance movement, explained it in these terms. The German people had 'either to hope for the defeat of their nation in order that Christian civilisation might survive, or to hope for victory entailing the destruction of our civilisation' (cited in Karl-Dietrich Bracher, 'Problems of the German Resistance', *The Challenge of the Third Reich* 1986, p. 67). The halo of patriotism which surrounded those who joined resistance movements in Europe was not accorded to Germans who worked for Hitler's downfall. They were more likely to be branded as traitors.

What kind of resistance was possible in a police state? Three main variants were attempted. There was the open protest in the form of speech and writing **[6.22]**, in the hope of influencing public opinion. This was rarely successful, and was attended with obvious risk. There was the possibility of exploiting the polycratic nature of the regime in order to modify the policies pursued, a technique that the *Abwehr* (The German military counter-intelligence organi-sation) under Admiral Canaris used successfully for a time. Finally there were the conspiratorial weapons of coup and assassination. In the documents which follow each of these variants is examined, along with the motives of those who were brave enough to pursue them.

Open protest

The churches' record of opposition to Hitler is a mixed one, but they provide the only example of corporate protest. Hitler had a number of dedicated supporters in the Lutheran Church who formed themselves into a distinct group, and took the name *Deutsche Christen*. It was one of their number, Ludwig Müller, who in a rigged election was made *Reichsbishop* in 1933. This led to the defection of about 2,000 Lutheran pastors who formed the Confessional Church, among them Martin Niemöller and Dietrich Bonhoeffer. The Confessional Church held its first synod in June 1934 at Barmen. It drew up six Articles of Faith, the fifth of which re-stated the relationship of church and state:

6.19

We reject the false doctrine that the state, over and above its special charge, should become the single and totalitarian order of human life, thus fulfilling the church's mission as well.

The German Resistance to Hitler, ed. H. Graml, M. Mommsen *et al.*, 1970, p. 214

Martin Niemöller also took the lead in opposing the extension of the Aryan clause to the Lutheran Church. This law, passed in 1933, banned those of the Jewish race from taking part in cultural activities. Niemöller was arrested in 1937 and remained in concentration camps until 1945.

The Twelfth Prussian Confessional Synod, held at Breslau on 16–17 October 1943, explicitly attacked the policies of extermination that had by now become evident on the Eastern Front:

6.20

Concepts such as 'extermination', 'liquidation', and 'useless life' are unknown in the divine order. The annihilation of people merely because they are old or mentally sick, or because they belong to another race, is a wielding of the sword that is not given to authority . . . Man's life belongs to God alone. It is sacred to Him, as are also the lives of the People of Israel.

The German Resistance to Hitler, ed. H. Graml, M. Mommsen *et al.*, 1970, p. 217

Hitler's Concordat with the Roman Catholic Church in 1933 effectively deprived the Roman Catholic Church of its political influence, and the Vatican continued to urge obedience to Hitler's regime, while protesting at some of its features. Individual Roman Catholics were prepared to challenge the state more openly. Father Delp and Father Roesch, both Jesuits, joined the *Kreisau* circle. Stauffenburg, a key figure in the bomb plot against Hitler, was also a Roman Catholic. The most successful open protest against Hitler's policies was the sermon preached against euthanasia by Graf Clemens August von Galen, Bishop of Münster, on 3 August 1941, from which the following extract is taken:

6.21

The Penal Code lays down in §139: 'He who receives credible information concerning the intention to commit a crime against life and neglects to alert the authorities or the person threatened in time . . . will be punished.' When I learnt of the intention to transport patients from Marienthal in order to kill them, I brought a formal charge at the State Court in Münster and with the Police President in   5
Münster by means of a registered letter which read as follows: 'According to information I have received, in the course of this week a large number of patients from the Marienthal Provincial Asylum near Münster are to be transported to the Eichberg asylum as so-called "unproductive national comrades" and will then soon be deliberately killed, as is generally believed has occurred with such transports   10
from other asylums. Since such an action is not only contrary to the moral laws of God and Nature but also is punishable with death as murder under §211 of the Penal Code, I hereby bring a charge in accordance with my duty under §219 of the Penal Code, and request you to provide immediate protection for the national comrades threatened in this way by taking action against those agencies who are   15
intending their removal and murder.

Nazism, 1919–1945, ed. J. Noakes and G. Pridham, vol. III, 1988, p. 1037

Galen's protest was so widely supported that Goebbels advised against his arrest, and the euthanasia programme was abandoned.

Perhaps the most outspoken and idealistic protesters against Hitler's rule were the students of Munich University who formed the White Rose movement. At its centre were Hans and Sophie Scholl and Christopher Probst. Hans Scholl was a medical student, as was Christopher Probst. They were supported by Kurt Huber, a Professor of Psychology and Philosophy. The Scholls began distributing leaflets condemning the regime in 1941, after receiving the text of Galen's sermon. Hans, who served as a medical orderly on the Eastern Front, was all too well aware of the atrocities that were taking place there against Jews and Russians. On his return to Munich his leaflets referred to these atrocities and the failure of the German people to do anything about them:

6.22

Why, in the face of all this abominable and inhuman crime is the German nation behaving so apathetically? Hardly anyone seems to worry about it. The situation is just accepted as such without further debate, and the German nation goes on sleeping its dull, stupid sleep, giving these Fascist criminals the boldness and opportunity to storm ahead – and they do.

Die Weisse Rose, ed. Inge Scholl, Fischer Verlag, 1955, p. 127, translated by M.J. Simpson

The Scholls distributed their final leaflet on 18 February 1943. The *Gestapo*, forewarned, were waiting for them, and they were arrested, together with Probst and Huber. All were tried for treason, found guilty and executed.

Questions

1 How do you account for the ambivalent attitude taken by the Roman Catholic and Lutheran Churches to Hitler?
2 Why do you think that Galen's protest about euthanasia [6.21] was successful, while the Twelfth Prussian Confessional Synod's objections to the liquidation of the Jews [6.20] had so little impact?
3 What was the significance of the White Rose movement?

Covert resistance

Resistance from within the regime came from generals such as Beck and Olbricht; members of the Foreign Office such as Weizsäcker; and, surprisingly, from members of the *Abwehr*, which somehow escaped Nazi domination until 1944. The dilemma confronting those who tried to oppose the regime from within is well illustrated in the different courses taken by two members of the Foreign Office, Ulrich von Hassell and Ernst von Weizsäcker. To leave government service meant ending any possibility of influencing policy. To stay on was to risk corruption. Hassell was ambassador in Rome from 1932 until his dismissal in February 1938. He joined the clandestine opposition to Hitler and was one of those put to death after the 1944 bomb plot. Weizsäcker, ambassador to Norway in 1933 and to Switzerland in 1937, accepted the post of State Secretary, when Ribbentrop became Foreign Minister in February 1938. He was demoted to become ambassador to the Vatican in 1943. Initially, Hassell and Weiszäcker were friends and colleagues, and co-operated to restrain Hitler. But as the war went on Hassell became increasingly disillusioned with Weizsäcker, who was ultimately tried as a war criminal and sentenced to five years' imprisonment, later commuted to one year. Hassell kept a secret diary, first published in 1948. Weizsäcker wrote his memoirs after the war. **6.23(a,b)** are drawn from these sources and illustrate the changes in their relationship.

6.23(a)   Extracts from Ulrich von Hassell's diaries

November 28, 1938
Had conversation with Professor A and M . . . as to what one could do to give public expression to the general abhorrence of these methods, unfortunately without success; without office we have no weapon. Any action on our part would lead to our being silenced – or worse. . .   5
April 20, 1943
W. has a post at the Vatican which could be important, but which it certainly is not under this regime. He merely lends himself to the Nazis as the usual false front.

Ulrich von Hassell, *Diaries*, 1948, pp. 22, 270

6.23(b)   Extract from Ernst von Weizsäcker's memoirs

In the winter of 1936–7 I felt pulled in two opposite directions: on the one side I had a feeling of aversion against a Foreign Office which at a time when such a dangerous course was being steered, had to such an extent allowed the rudder to be taken from its hands; and on the other side I felt drawn to the office because in such a time of crises it was most dependent on its solid core of officials, and to have left it   5
now would have been equivalent to desertion . . . It is just this instability of Ribbentrop's which seems to me to provide one with the freedom of movement needed to fulfil the task – the only task for which I am taking up this cross – of preventing war. [Marginal note made at the time on appointment as State Secretary, March 1938.]

Ernst von Weizsäcker, *Memoirs*, translated by John Andrews, 1951, p. 108

Attempts to remove Hitler by force

At the head of the *Abwehr* was Admiral Canaris, and both he and his deputy, Hans Oster, worked to bring about Hitler's downfall. The *Abwehr* also provided an asylum for men like Hans von Dohnanyi and Dietrich Bonhoeffer, who were able to work under its protection.

The main efforts of these men were initially directed at preventing the war, and, once it had broken out, at bringing it to an end. General Beck, when he learned of Hitler's plans to invade Czechoslovakia in 1938, did his best to convince his fellow generals of the wrongness of such a course. When he failed, he resigned. A plan was then hatched with Oster and Dohnanyi to have Hitler arrested and tried by a People's Court for endangering the safety of Germany. Various emissaries were sent to England in August and September 1938 to persuade British politicians of the seriousness of Hitler's intentions. One of those sent was Major von Kleist, a close friend of Canaris. But he had a very lukewarm reaction in Britain [6.24] and the Munich Agreement put paid to any hopes of a successful coup. British scepticism about the sincerity and effectiveness of the opposition to Hitler at this point is well illustrated in the following source:

6.24   Chamberlain's comment on Kleist, 19 August 1938

I take it that von Kleist is violently anti-Hitler and is extremely anxious to stir up his friends in Germany to make an attempt at [the regime's] overthrow. He reminds me of the Jacobites at the Court of France in King William's time, and I think we must discount a good deal of what he says.

R. Manvell and H. Fraenkel, *The Canaris Conspiracy*, 1969, p. 37

After the outbreak of war, links with Britain were maintained through the activities of men like Bonhoeffer, who met Bishop Bell of Chichester in Sweden in May 1942, and Adam von Trott, who communicated with Sir Stafford Cripps through Dr Visser 't Hooft, secretary of a Protestant oecumenical organisation in Geneva. Trott drew up a memorandum dated April 1942, which reflected the views of the Kreisau circle at the time [6.25].

Trott was suspected of being a Nazi agent, unjustifiably, and in any case there was little prospect of the British government entering into serious negotiations with any group until Hitler had been removed. What really cut the ground from under the feet of these men's efforts was the announcement after the Casablanca Conference in January 1943 that the Allies would insist on the 'unconditional surrender' of Germany, Italy and Japan. From that point on Hitler's opponents knew that even should they succeed in removing the Führer they would be in no position to negotiate peace terms. Whether such a prospect was ever a realistic one may perhaps be judged from the terms of the Trott Memorandum.

6.25   The Trott Memorandum

'The most urgent and immediate task to stave off catastrophe is the earliest possible
overthrow of the Regime of Germany.'

Trott emphasised the Christian essence of the anti-Nazi opposition and indicated
the obstacles it had to face, including 'the complete uncertainty of the British and
American attitude towards a change of government in Germany', and fear of   5
'movements of indiscriminate hatred' against Germans of all kinds. He urged a
decentralised form of government in Germany and a federal structure for Europe.

Where Germany's frontiers were concerned he stated: 'We believe in the
necessity to reconstitute a free Polish and Czech state within the limits of their
ethnographic frontiers.'   10

He concluded: 'An exchange of ideas seems to us hopeless only as long as we are
faced with a one-sided tendency to blame and judge.'

C. Sykes, *Troubled Loyalty, A Biography of Adam von Trott,* **1968, pp. 378–9**

Despite the refusal of the Allies to consider negotiating with Hitler's opponents, by 1942 many of his generals were convinced that Hitler's assassination
was now the only course open to them. Plans were first drawn up in the autumn
of that year by Generals Beck, Olbricht and Tresckow. There were two
unsuccessful attempts on Hitler's life in March and November 1943 respectively. The bomb plot of 20 July 1944 was an altogether more ambitious affair.
Some 200 important figures were directly implicated, including 19 generals, 26
colonels and lieutenant colonels, 7 diplomats, 2 ambassadors, 1 minister, 3 state
secretaries and the Chief of the Criminal Police (figures from *Die Zeit*, 21 July
1989). The story of the plot and its failure has been told often enough. What
perhaps needs to be stressed is the scale of the conspiracy and the motives of
those involved. The official list of those executed after the plot runs to 5,746.
Tresckow, who was a general on the Eastern Front at the time, and
Stauffenberg, who actually delivered the bomb, explain their actions in **6.26**
and **6.27**. Tresckow, after hearing news of the Allied invasion on 6 June wrote:

6.26

The assassination must be attempted at any cost. Even should that fail, the attempt
to seize power in the capital must be undertaken. We must prove to the world and
to future generations that the men of the German resistance movement dared to
take the decisive step and to hazard their lives upon it. Compared with this, nothing
else matters.

R. Manvell and H. Fraenkel, *The Canaris Conspiracy,* **1969, p. 181**

Shortly before 20 July 1944 Stauffenburg wrote:

6.27

It is time that something is done. But whoever dares to act must realise that he will probably go down in German history as a traitor. Yet if he fails to act, he will be a traitor to his own conscience.

The German Resistance to Hitler, ed. H. Graml and M. Mommsen *et al.*, 1970, p. 232

Dietrich Bonhoeffer, who was in prison on 20 July 1944, justified his association with the plots against Hitler in these terms:

6.28

If a lunatic tears through the streets in his car, as a pastor on the scene I cannot only comfort and bury those who have been run over, but I must jump in and stop him.

Die Zeit, 21 July 1989

Questions

1 Was Weizsäcker a victim of self-delusion or was he right to accept promotion in 1938 [6.23]?
2 Explain Chamberlain's reference to the 'Jacobites at the Court of France' [6.24]. Do you think the analogy he draws is a fair one?
3 Does the Trott Memorandum [6.25] support the view that British and American governments were justified in demanding the unconditional surrender of Germany?
4 'The time will come when men will be ashamed to admit that they were part of the 20 July *putsch*' (Major General Remer, colonel of the battalion that arrested some of the July plotters in Berlin, speaking in 1951).
   'The act of 20 July 1944 – an act directed against wrong and unfreedom – is a shining light in Germany's darkest hour' (Order of the Day, General Heusinger, head of the German army, in 1959).
   Under what circumstances are men justified in attempting to overthrow governments by force? Did such conditions exist in Germany in 1944?
5 For general discussion: How was it possible for a civilised country to fall prey for twelve years to a man of Hitler's character and outlook?

Bibliography

Bibliographical
J. Hiden and J. Farquharson, *Explaining the Third Reich, Historians and the Third Reich*, Batsford, 1989

Source material
Norman H. Baynes (ed.), *The Speeches of Adolf Hitler, 1922–1939*, 2 vols., Oxford University Press, 1942
Documents on British Foreign Policy, 1919–1939, second series, vols. XII–XIX, HMSO, 1972–83
Adolf Hitler, *Mein Kampf*, translated by Ralph Mannheim, Hutchinson, 1969
J. Noakes and G. Pridham (eds.), *Nazism, 1919–1945*: vol. I *The Rise to Power, 1919–1934*, Exeter University Press, 1983; vol. II *State, Economy and Society*, Exeter University Press, 1984; vol. III *Foreign Policy, War and Extermination*, Exeter University Press, 1988
Telford Taylor (ed.), *Hitler's Secret Book*, Grove Press, New York, 1961
Questions on German History: Ideas, Forces, Decisions from 1800 to the Present, Historical Exhibition in the Berlin Reichstag Catalogue, 9th (updated) edition, German Bundestag and Press Information, Publications Section, Bonn, 1984

General background
V.R. Berghahn, *Modern Germany*, Cambridge University Press, 1982
H. Bull (ed.), *The Challenge of the Third Reich*, Clarendon Press, 1986
G.A. Craig, *Germany, 1866–1945*, Oxford University Press, 1978
Ian Kershaw, *The Nazi Dictatorship*, Arnold, 1985, second edition 1989
J. Taylor and W. Shaw, *A Dictionary of the Third Reich*, Collins, 1987

The Weimar Republic and the peace settlements
A. Adamthwaite, *The Lost Peace: International Relations in Europe, 1919–1939*, Arnold, 1980
R. Brunet, *The German Constitution*, T. Fisher Unwin, 1923
E. Eyck, *A History of the Weimar Republic*, 2 vols., J. Wiley, 1967
J.W. Hiden, *The Weimar Republic*, Longman, 1974
A. Luckau, *The German Delegation at the Paris Peace Conference*, Columbia University Press, 1941
H. Nicolson, *Peacemaking 1919*, Methuen, 1964
H.A. Turner, *Stresemann and the Politics of the Weimar Republic*, Princeton University Press, 1963
R.M. Watt, *The Kings Depart*, Pelican Books, 1973

Nazism
Theodore Abel, *Why Hitler Came into Power*, Harvard University Press, 1986
K.D. Bracher, *The German Dictatorship*, Penguin, 1973
A. Bullock, *Hitler, A Study in Tyranny*, Penguin, 1962
W. Carr, *Hitler, A Study in Personality and Politics*, Arnold, 1978
J.C. Fest, *Hitler*, Penguin, 1977
M. Kater, *The Nazi Party, A Social Profile of Members and Leaders, 1919–1945*, Blackwell, 1983
Kurt G.W. Ludecke, *I Knew Hitler*, C. Scribner, 1938
W.L. Shirer, *The Rise and Fall of the Third Reich*, Secker and Warburg, 1960

The collapse of the Weimar Republic
D. Abraham, *The Collapse of the Weimar Republic*, Princeton University Press, 1982
F.L. Carsten, *The Reichswehr and Politics, 1918–1933*, Oxford University Press, 1966

T. Childers, *The Nazi Voter, The Social Foundations of Fascism, 1919–1933*, University of North Carolina Press, 1985
Rudolf Herberle, *From Democracy to Nazism*, Howard Fertig, 1970
R.N. Hunt, *German Social Democracy*, Yale University Press, New Haven, 1964
H. James, *The German Slump, Politics and Economics, 1924–1936*, Clarendon Press, 1986
H.W. Koch (ed.), *Aspects of the Third Reich*, Macmillan, 1985
R. Manvell and H. Fraenkel, *The Hundred Days to Hitler*, Dent, 1974
R.J. Overy, *The Nazi Economic Recovery, 1932–1938*, Macmillan, 1982
H.A. Winkler, 'German Society and the Illusion of Restoration', *Journal of Modern History*, October 1976

The Nazi regime at home
B. Engelmann, *In Hitler's Germany*, Methuen, 1988
J.C. Fest, *The Face of the Third Reich*, Penguin, 1979
R. Grunberger, *A Social History of the Third Reich*, Penguin, 1971
Ian Kershaw, *The Nazi Dictatorship*, chapters 3 and 4 (see above)
F. Neumann, *Behemoth: the Structure and Practice of National Socialism*, Cass, 1967
R.J. Overy, *The Nazi Economic Recovery, 1932–1938* (see above)
A. Speer, *Inside the Third Reich*, Weidenfeld and Nicolson, 1970
J. Stern, *Hitler, The Führer and the People*, Fontana, 1975
D.G. Williamson, *The Third Reich*, Longman, 1982

Foreign policy
R. Cecil, *Hitler's Decision to Invade Russia*, Davis-Poynter, 1975
F. Fischer, *Germany's Aims in the First World War*, Chatto and Windus, 1967
F. Fischer, *From Kaisserreich to Third Reich; Elements of Continuity in German History, 1871–1945*, Allen and Unwin, 1986
H.W. Koch, 'Hitler's "Programme" and the Genesis of Operation "Barbarossa"', in *Aspects of the Third Reich* (see above)
G. Martel (ed.), *'The Origins of the Second World War' Reconsidered*, Unwin Hyman, 1986
W. Michalka, 'From the Anti-Comintern Pact to the Euro-Asiatic Bloc, Ribbentrop's Alternative Concept to Hitler's Foreign Policy Programme', in *Aspects of the Third Reich* (see above)
E.M. Robertson (ed.), *The Origins of the Second World War*, Macmillan, 1971
A.J.P. Taylor, *The Origins of the Second World War*, Penguin, 1964
D.C. Watt, *How War Came*, Heinemann, 1989

German responses to Hitler
M. Balfour, *Withstanding Hitler's Germany 1933–45*, Routledge and Kegan Paul, 1988
R. Bessel, *Life in the Third Reich*, Oxford University Press, 1987
C. Bielenburg, *The Past is Myself*, Corgi Books, 1984
K.D. Bracher, 'Problems of the German Resistance', in *The Challenge of the Third Reich*, ed. H. Bull, Clarendon Press, 1986
M. Broszat, 'The Genesis of the Final Solution', in *Aspects of the Third Reich* (see above)
B. Engelmann, *In Hitler's Germany* (see above)
G. Fleming, *The Final Solution*, Oxford University Press, 1986
H. Graml, M. Mommsen *et al.*, *The German Resistance to Hitler*, Batsford, 1970
T.W. Mason, 'The Third Reich and the German Left: Persecution and Resistance', in *The Challenge of the Third Reich*, ed. H. Bull, Clarendon Press, 1986
H. Mommsen, 'Anti-Jewish Politics and the Implementation of the Holocaust', in *The Challenge of the Third Reich*, ed. H. Bull, Clarendon Press, 1986
T. Prittie, *Germans against Hitler*, Hutchinson, 1964

Acknowledgements

The author and publisher are grateful to the following for permission to reproduce extracts and illustrations:

Extracts 1.4, 1.9 R.M. Watt, *The Kings Depart*, 1973, by permission of International Creative Management, Inc; 1.5, 3.10 E. Eyck, *A History of the Weimar Republic*, vols. I–II, 1967, by permission of Harvard University Press; 1.7(a–c) H.A. Turner, *Stresemann and the Politics of the Weimar Republic*, 1963, Princeton University Press; 1.8 L. Hertzman, *DNVP: Right-Wing Opposition in the Weimar Republic 1918–1924*, 1963, University of Nebraska Press; 1.10, 3.5, 3.7 R.N. Hunt, *German Social Democracy 1918–1933*, 1964, © Yale University Press; 1.11(a) H. Nicolson, *Peacemaking 1919*, 1964, Methuen, London; 1.14 K. Epstein, *Matthias Erzberger, A Dilemma of German Democracy*, 1957, Princeton University Press; 1.16. 3.4(c) V. Schiff, *The Germans at Versailles 1919*, 1930 published by Williams and Norgate, Ernest Benn, A & C Black; 1.19 A. Joseph Berlau, *The German Social Democratic Party*, 1949, by permission of Octagon Books, a division of Hippocrene Books, Inc.; 1.20 R.H. Samuel and R. Hinton Thomas, *Education and Society in Modern Germany*, 1949, Routledge; 2.1 J.G. Fichte, *Addresses to the German Nation*, 1922, Open Court Publishing Company, a subsidiary of Carus Corporation; 2.2 extract taken from *Bismarck, The Story of a Fighter* by Emil Ludwig, reproduced by kind permission of Unwin Hyman Ltd; 2.3 H.U. Wehler, *The German Empire 1871–1918*, 1985, Berg; 2.4 Hans Kohn, *The Mind of Germany: The Education of a Nation*, Charles Scribner's Sons, 1960. Reprinted by permission; 2.5 H.S. Chamberlain, *Foundations of the Nineteenth Century*, translated by J. Lees, vol. 1, 1909. Bodley Head; 2.8, 2.13, 3.16. 6.10 Norman Baynes (ed.), *The Speeches of Adolf Hitler, April 1922–August 1939*, vol. 1, 1942, published by Oxford University Press for the Royal Institute of International Affairs, London; 2.10, 2.11, 5.1(a, b, di), 6.1, 6.14(a) Adolf Hitler, *Mein Kampf*, translated by Ralph Manheim. Copyright 1943 and copyright © renewed 1971 by Houghton Mifflin Co. Reprinted by permission of Houghton Mifflin Co. and Hutchinson; 2.12, 3.6(a), 3.12(b), 3.13, 4.6, 4.7, 4.11, 4.12, 4.17(c), 4.21, 4.22, 4.23, 4.24(a), 5.2, 5.3, 5.5, 5.7, 5.9. 5.21, 5.22, 5.24, 6.2, 6.4, 6.7, 6.12, 6.14(b), 6.15, 6.16, 6.17(a), 6.21 J. Noakes and G. Pridham (eds.), *Nazism 1919–1945: A History of Documents and Eyewitness Accounts*, vols 1–3. Copyright © 1983, 1984 by Department of History and Archaeology, University of Exeter. Reprinted by permission of Pantheon Books, a division of Random House, Inc.; 2.14 Kurt Ludecke, *I Knew Hitler*, 1938, Hutchinson; 2.17 M. Kater, *The Nazi Party, A Social Profile of Members and Leaders, 1919–1945*, 1983, Basil Blackwell; 2.18 Theodore Abel, *Why Hitler Came to Power*, © 1966, 1938, reprinted by permission of the publisher, Prentice Hall, a division of Simon & Schuster, Englewood Cliffs, N.J. 07632; 3.1(a, b), 3.3 V.R. Berghahn, *Modern Germany*, 1982, Cambridge University Press; 3.1(c) H. James, *The German Slump, Politics and Economics, 1924–1936*, 1986, by permission of the Oxford University Press; 3.2 D. Abraham, *The Collapse of the Weimar Republic*, by permission of the author; 3.4(a) G.A. Craig, *Germany, 1866–1945*, 1978, by permission of the Oxford University Press; 3.4(b), 3.11 F.L. Carsten, *The Reichswehr and Politics 1918–33*, 1966, Oxford University Press; 3.8, 4.17(a–b) R.J. Overy, *The Nazi Economic Recovery 1932–1938*, 1982, by permission of Macmillan, London and Basingstoke; 3.9 G.A. Craig, *Germany 1866–1945*, 1978 Oxford University Press; 3.15 T. Childers, *The Nazi Voter: The Social Foundations of Facism in Germany, 1919–1933*. © 1983 The University of North Carolina Press. Reprinted by permission; 3.17 R. Manvell and H. Fraenkel, *The Hundred Days to Hitler*, 1974, J.M. Dent; 4.1 M. Domarus, *Hitler, Reden und Proklamationen, 1932–45*, vol. 1, 1962, Pamminger & Partner Verlagsgesellschaft MBH; 4.13 A. Bullock, *Hitler, A Study in Tyranny*, 1962, by permission of Paul Hamlyn Publishing, part of Reed International Books, and Harper Collins Publishers; 4.14, 5.18, 5.20 A. Speer, *Inside the Third Reich*, 1970, George Weidenfeld and Nicholson Ltd; 4.16, 5.6, 5.8, 5.11, 5.13, 5.14, 5.16, 5.27 J. Noakes and G. Pridham (eds.), *Nazism, 1919–1945*, by permission of Her Majesty's Stationery Office; 4.26(b), 6.11, 6.13(a) Bernt Engelmann, *In Hitler's Germany*, Methuen, London. English translation copyright © 1986 by Random House Inc. Reprinted by permission of the Octopus Publishing Group Library and Pantheon Books, a division of Random House Inc.; 5.4, 5.19, 5.23, 5.25 H.W. Koch (ed.), *Aspects of the Third Reich*, 1985, by permission of Macmillan, London and Basingstoke and St. Martin's Press Inc. © W. Michalka, Chapter 9-1985, and © H.W. Koch, Chapter, 10-1985. c/o St Martin's Press, 175 Fifth Avenue, New York, NY 10010; 5.12 extract taken from *The Origins of the Second World War Reconsidered*, edited by G. Martel, reproduced by kind permission of Unwin Hyman Ltd; 5.15(a) reprinted from *How War Came* by Donald Cameron Watt, by permission of William Heinemann Limited and Pantheon Books, a division of Random House, Inc. Copyright © 1989 by Donald Cameron Watt; 5.17 C.J. Burckhardt, *Meine Danziger Mission 1937–1939*, 1962, © Verlag Georg D.W. Callwey; 6.5, 6.6 from the Archives of the Dachau Concentration Camp Memorial; 6.8, 6.13(c) R. Bessel, *Life in the Third Reich*, 1987, Oxford University Press; 6.9 speech by Philip Jenninger, by permission of the Guardian News Service Ltd; 6.13(b), 6.18 © Christabel Bielenberg 1970. Extracted from *The Past is Myself*, published by Corgi Books, a division of Transworld Publishers Ltd. All rights reserved; 6.13(d) Mathilde Wolff-Monckeberg, *On the Other Side, to My Children; from Germany, 1940–45*, translated and edited by Ruth Evans, 1979, Peter Owen Ltd; 6.17(b) G. Fleming, *Hitler and the Final Solution*, University of California Press Copyright © 1984; 6.19, 6.20, 6.27 H. Graml, Mommsen *et al.* (eds.), *The German Resistance to Hitler*, 1970, Batsford; 6.22 Inge Scholl, *Die Weisse Rose* (English version entitled *The White Rose*, Wesleyan University Press), © 1952 by Inge Aicher-Scholl, reprinted with permission of Liepman AG, Zürich; 6.23(b) Ernst von Weizsäcker, *Memoirs*, translated by John Andrews, 1951, Victor Gollancz Ltd; 6.24, 6.26 R. Manvell and H. Fraenkel, *The Canaris Conspiracy*, William Heinemann; 6.25 C. Sykes, *Troubled Loyalty. A Bibliography of Adam von Trott*, 1968, by permission of Peters, Fraser & Dunlop; 6.28 passage from *Abschniedsbriefe und Aufzeichnungen des Widerstandes 1933–1945*, by permission of *Die Zeit*.

Illustrations 1.2(b) W.O. Simpson, *Changing Horizon*, 1986, Stanley Thornes; 2.9(b) Weimar Archive; 3.6(b) Bundesarchiv Koblenz; 3.12(a) J. Noakes and G. Pridham (eds.), *Nazism, 1919–1945*, 1983, University of Exeter Press; 4.8(b), 4.18 Bayerischen Staatsbibliothek, Munich; 4.10 and cover illustration, 4.20 by permission of the Trustees of the Imperial War Museum; 5.15(b) *Rendezvous*, cartoon by David Low, Centre for the Study of Cartoons and Caricature, University of Kent at Canterbury, © Solo Syndication & Literary Agency Ltd; 6.3(b) photo taken by the Agentur Weltbild GmbH, reproduced by permission of Ullstein.

Every effort has been made to reach copyright holders; the publishers would like to hear from anyone whose rights they have unwittingly infringed.

Index